Tourism and Hospitality Management Series

Series Editors:

Stephen J. Page
Massey University – Albany, New Zealand

Professor Roy C. Wood
The Scottish Hotel School, University of Strathclyde, UK

Series Consultant:

Professor C. L. Jenkins
The Scottish Hotel School, University of Strathclyde, UK

Textbooks in this series:

Books in this series are available on free inspection for lecturers considering the texts for course adoption. Details of these and any other International Thomson Business Press titles are available by writing to the publishers (Berkshire House, 168–173 High Holborn, London WCIV 7AA) or by telephoning the Promotions Department on 0171 497 1422

Rural Tourism
An Introduction

Richard and Julia Sharpley

INTERNATIONAL THOMSON BUSINESS PRESS
I ⓉP® An International Thomson Publishing Company

London • Bonn • Boston • Johannesburg • Madrid • Melbourne • Mexico City • New York • Paris
Singapore • Tokyo • Toronto • Albany, NY • Belmont, CA • Cincinnati, OH • Detroit, MI

Rural Tourism: An Introduction

Copyright ©1997 Richard and Julia Sharpley

First published by International Thomson Business Press

I(T)P® A division of International Thomson Publishing Inc.
The ITP logo is a trademark under licence

British Library Cataloguing-in-Publication Data
A catalogue record for this book is available from the British Library

Library of Congress Cataloging-in-Publication Data
A catalog record for this book is available from the Library of Congress

First edition 1997

Typeset by J&L Composition Ltd, Filey, North Yorkshire
Printed in the UK by the Alden Press, Oxford

ISBN 0 415 1401 02

International Thomson Business Press
Berkshire House
168–173 High Holborn
London WCIV 7AA
UK

International Thomson Business Press
20 Park Plaza
13th Floor
Boston MA 02116
USA

http://www.itbp.com

To
Janet and John Mitchell

Contents

Acknowledgements

We are very grateful to a number of colleagues who have allowed us to draw upon their ideas and knowledge, including Lesley Roberts, Carolyn Spencer, Rory Maclellan, Sandra Carey, Peter Grabowski, Brandon Crimes, Sean Gammon and Scott McCabe.

We would also like to thank the following for permission to use tables and figures in the text: the Council of Europe for permission to reproduce Table 1.1; the English Tourist Board for permission to reproduce Figure 1.2; Travel and Tourism Intelligence (formerly the travel and tourism division of the Economist Intelligence Unit) for permission to reproduce Table 1.2; the OECD for permission to reproduce Table 2.2; Elsevier Science Ltd, Kidlington, UK, for permission to reproduce Table 2.3; Bord Fáilte for permission to reproduce Table 2.4; Channel View Books for permission to reproduce Table 1.3 and Figure 5.6; Butterworth–Heinemann for permission to reproduce Figure 5.1; and Addison Wesley Longman Ltd. for permission to reproduce Table 5.1 and Figure 5.2.

Whilst every effort has been made to seek permission from copyright holders, we apologise for any unknowing use of copyright material. In such cases, could the owners please contact the authors via the publishers.

Richard and Julia Sharpley

Abbreviations

ADAS	Agricultural and Development Advice Service
ADT	Australia Department of Tourism
ANTREC	National Association of Rural, Ecological and Cultural Tourism
CAP	Common Agricultural Policy
CIM	Chartered Institute of Marketing
CPRE	Campaign for the Protection of Rural England
CRN	Countryside Recreation Network
CTAP	Community Tourism Action Plan
CTB	Cumbria Tourist Board
CTO	Cyprus Tourist Board
DoE	Department of the Environment
EAGGF	European Agricultural Guidance and Guarantee Fund
EC	European Community
EIU	European Intelligence Unit
ERDF	European Regional Development Fund
ESAs	Environmentally Sensitive Areas
ESF	European Social Fund
ETB	English Tourist Board
EU	European Union
EUROTER	European rural tourism organisation (sponsored by Council of Europe)
FNNPE	Federation of Nature and National Parks of Europe
GDP	Gross Domestic Product
IUCN	International Union for the Conservation of Nature
LEADER	Liaisons Entre Actions pour la Développement des Economies Rurales
MAFF	Ministry of Agriculture, Fisheries and Food
OECD	Organisation for Economic Co-operation and Development
Our-TOWN	On-line Recreation and Tourism Opportunities Network
SPARC	South Pembrokeshire Partnership for Action with Rural Communities
TCRI	Taf and Cleddau Rural Initiative
TCTA	Tarka Country Tourist Association
TER	L'Association Tourisme en Espace Rural
USTTA	United States Travel and Tourism Administration
VFR	Visiting Friends and Relatives
WCED	World Commission on Environment and Development
WTO	World Tourism Organisation
WTTC	World Travel and Tourism Council

Figures

Tables

Introduction

There can be no doubting the importance of rural tourism. For almost 200 years, since the early tourists first ventured into alpine Europe, the wilderness of the American west or the British highlands, rural areas have attracted ever increasing numbers of visitors and, in many countries, it is now one of the most popular forms of tourism. In the United States, for example, it is estimated that over 70 per cent of the population enjoy some form of rural recreation (OECD 1993), a figure largely mirrored throughout the industrialised world, whilst a recent survey in the United Kingdom revealed that over 900 million day visits alone were made to the countryside in 1993 (CRN 1994). More generally, throughout Europe, about a quarter of the population spend their main holiday in a countryside destination; this rises to about one third when short breaks and second holidays are considered (Davidson 1992:142) and, in both cases, the figures are doubled when mountain areas are included as tourist destinations.

Nor is it simply the level of participation in rural tourism that has rapidly increased, particularly since the 1950s. The range of activities that comprise rural tourism has also expanded dramatically, increasing the opportunities for people to visit the countryside. Thus, although traditional activities, such as hiking, climbing and camping, remain popular, technological advances and higher levels of disposable income have allowed more people to participate in a greater variety of pursuits; in the UK, for example, at least twenty-eight categories of countryside sport are officially recognised (Sports Council 1991), including a variety of 'modern' sports, such as mountain-biking, off-road driving and hang-gliding.

As impressive as these statistics are, however, the real significance of rural tourism only becomes apparent when it is studied in the context of all tourism and from a broader social and economic perspective. In other words, there is little to be gained from examining rural tourism in isolation, without considering the wider, external factors which, on the one hand, have influenced the growth in the level and scope of participation in rural tourism and, on the other hand, have strengthened the role of tourism in the socio-economic regeneration and diversification of rural areas.

For example, it has long been recognised that a positive relationship exists between the growth of rural tourism and broader developments and changes in society as a whole. The notion of rural tourism, of visiting rural areas for leisure purposes, first emerged as a result of the rapid industrialisation and urbanisation of Western societies during the nineteenth century and, whilst other factors, such as improvements in transport and increased wealth and free time, enabled people to visit the countryside in greater numbers, it was essentially the transformation of society from a rural to a predominantly urban structure that provided the initial incentive for the development of rural tourism. More recent social and cultural changes, such as a greater interest in heritage, environmental concerns, the move towards healthier life styles and a rejection of the mass consumer culture of the 1960s and 1970s, have also heightened interest and participation in more specialist, individualistic and authentic forms of tourism, including rural tourism. Thus, the social and cultural context of the countryside as a tourist destination cannot be ignored.

Ironically, however, these trends and changes which were the initial catalyst for the emergence and growth of rural tourism have also contributed to a set of problems experienced by most, if not all, rural areas in the developed world. As a result of urbanisation, industrialisation and continuing technological advance, many rural areas have suffered a fundamental transformation of their economic and social structures. In particular, employment opportunities in agriculture have been dramatically reduced whilst most rural areas have experienced falling incomes, a decline in local services such as shops, schools, libraries and transport services, increasingly aged populations and, overall, a loss of traditional rural culture. In some areas these trends have been halted by counter-urbanisation; many rural settlements now form part of the commuter belt surrounding larger towns and cities but, in the more remote, marginal areas, the development of rural tourism is seen by both local communities and policy makers as a primary force in the revitalisation of rural areas. In other words, rural tourism, as a perceived panacea for the economic and social problems facing many rural communities, has become inextricably linked with broader development plans and policies.

In short, rural tourism is a complex and diverse area of study. It encompasses a variety of issues, problems and challenges faced, to a lesser or greater extent, by rural areas in many parts of the world and, as an introduction to the study of rural tourism, this book draws together many of these issues. It examines the growth and development of, and the demand for, rural tourism as a specific sector of the overall tourism market and it considers the role and potential of tourism in the socio-economic development and regeneration of rural areas. The overall objective of the book is to demonstrate and explain the way in which rural tourism is inextricably linked to the resource upon which it depends and, hence, the necessity for an integrated and sustainable approach to the development; marketing, planning and management issues are, therefore, also covered. Throughout the book reference is made to relevant articles and books to facilitate more in-depth study of specific topics and issues and a short list of suggested titles for further reading is included at the end of each chapter.

In order to 'set the scene', Chapter 1 introduces the concept of rural tourism, highlighting those characteristics which identify it as a separate segment of the overall tourism market and considering what is meant by the term 'countryside' as the setting for rural tourism. In Chapter 2, the multi-purpose nature of the countryside resource is examined, emphasising the notion that tourism is just one of a number of valid and viable demands on the resource. Particular attention is paid to the relationship between tourism and agricultural policies and the way in which tourism is becoming the new 'cash crop' in many rural areas. Chapter 3 considers the demand for rural tourism, describing the historical growth of rural tourism and analysing the factors and characteristics of the demand and motivation for rural tourism. This is followed, in Chapter 4, by an assessment of the supply of rural tourism from the point of view of, separately, the public and private sectors, concentrating in particular on public sector provision of recreational opportunities in rural areas and introducing the concept of the 'total rural tourism product'. The marketing of rural tourism is then examined in Chapter 5, the main concern being the difficult but, nevertheless, necessary task of applying a variety of marketing techniques to rural tourism and the benefits of doing so. In Chapter 6, the need for effective planning and management is emphasised and an outline planning process is suggested before the concept of sustainable tourism development is introduced. Finally, Chapter 7 considers a number of specific issues concerned with the current and future management of rural tourism, including access issues, second-home ownership and the impact of urbanisation on rural society and its values.

1 Understanding rural tourism

INTRODUCTION

'Is no nook of England secure from rash assault?' Concerned about the impact that the building of a railway to Windermere would have on the Lake District in north-west England, William Wordsworth wrote these words in 1844. More than 150 years later his fears have been largely confirmed; not only has much of England, but also most of the countryside throughout the developed world, succumbed to this so-called 'rash assault'.

Wordsworth was, of course, referring to tourism. During the second half of the eighteenth century relatively few people had the means, the time or even the inclination to participate in tourism. Travel was slow, uncomfortable and frequently dangerous. Furthermore, for those prepared to endure these hardships, the countryside in particular remained somewhere to be avoided rather than visited. However, by the 1840s railways were being constructed throughout Europe and north America, opening up, as Wordsworth feared, the more remote and beautiful rural areas to the travelling public. Higher levels of income and more free time meant that the populations of the new industrial towns and cities were increasingly able to visit the countryside and, by the turn of the century, many rural areas were benefiting from a thriving and established tourism industry.

Nowadays, the great majority of people in Western, industrialised nations participate in rural tourism at some time or another. For some, it may represent only an occasional visit lasting just a few hours, for others it might be a regular main holiday destination. Overall, however, rural tourism is a major growth sector of both domestic and international tourism markets (Lane 1994a). It is a significant source of employment and income, it can be an important vehicle for the socio-economic development of rural communities (Greffe 1994; Luloff *et al.* 1994), in many countries it is linked with agricultural policies, and it is frequently promoted as a means of conserving rural environments and culture (ETB 1988; Grahn 1991). Inevitably, perhaps, tourism also plays a pivotal role in the debates about the extent to which rural areas should be developed or conserved.

All of these themes are implicit in the study of rural tourism and are discussed in later chapters. However, it is important to consider first a number of basic issues and, in particular, to attempt to clarify what is meant by the term 'rural tourism'.

WHAT IS RURAL TOURISM?

Given both its importance as a widespread tourist activity and the growing emphasis placed upon it within local and regional development policies, it would be logical to assume that there is a commonly accepted definition of rural tourism. More specifically, it would justifiable to assume that there are identifiable characteristics, such as particular activities or locations, which clearly set rural tourism apart from other categories or forms of tourism. Surprisingly, however, no such definition or agreed set of characteristics exists.

At first sight, attempting to define rural tourism would seem to be an easy task. It is, as Lane (1994a) suggests, 'tourism which takes place in the countryside', but even this simple statement contains a number of ambiguities. For example, definitions of tourism itself can vary and, particularly within the context of the countryside, the distinction between activities which are strictly forms of tourism, leisure or sport can often be blurred. At the same time, it is equally difficult to define what is meant by 'countryside' or 'rural areas'. As is discussed shortly, many countries have differing criteria by which areas are judged to be rural or non-rural (i.e. urban), whilst 'rural' can be both a geographical definition and a description of the cultural characteristics of societies and communities in the countryside.

To compound the problem further, the term 'rural tourism' is frequently used inter-changeably with other terms, such as ecotourism, green tourism or nature tourism (see Whelan 1991). In some cases, this means that rural tourism is equated with specific activities or locations, such as farm tourism, whereas, in other cases, rural tourism is often used as a means of describing a more general, broader approach to tourism development and promotion. In Cyprus, for example, the Cyprus Tourism Organisation (CTO) is actively promoting the development of what it calls 'agritourism' to underpin the sustainable social and economic development of inland, rural areas which have not benefited from the rapid expansion of traditional beach tourism on the coast (see Case study 1).

In short, a variety of meanings or definitions may be attached to rural tourism and it is unlikely, therefore, that a single, satisfactory answer to the question 'what is rural tourism?' can be found. However, a clearer picture emerges if a number of points are addressed, in particular:

● what is the scope of rural tourism?
● is it possible to define 'countryside'?
● to what extent does the countryside possess social and cultural significance?
● is rural tourism simply one sector of the tourism market or does it represent a set of principles for the planning and development of tourism?

It is important to note that, given the introductory nature of this book, it is only possible to scratch at the surface of these issues, although more in depth analyses may be found elsewhere. For example, in recent years there has been a lively debate in the rural sociology literature concerning sociological definitions and meanings of rurality (Halfacree 1995). Never-the-less, a brief overview of the main points will provide a working definition of rural tourism to be used throughout this book.

THE SCOPE OF RURAL TOURISM

Visitors to the countryside participate in an enormous number and variety of activities. Some of these, such as walking or pony-trekking holidays, are clearly forms of tourism, whereas other pursuits are, perhaps, more commonly considered to be either leisure or sport. For example, mountaineering, caving, watching a sporting event in the countryside, or even simply visiting a country pub or restaurant, might normally be included in the latter categories. At the same time, not all tourism which occurs in rural areas can be described as being traditionally rural in character; that is, some tourism developments, such as theme parks or holiday villages, bear little relation to, and contrast starkly with, the rural environment (Clark *et al.* 1994; Lane 1994a).

Initially, therefore, it could be argued that the scope of rural tourism, or the range of activities or forms of tourism that comprise rural tourism, is somewhat limited. It is restricted by factors such as length of stay, length of journey, the form of activity, the type and size of attraction or facility, the location and, undoubtedly, by individual perceptions of what is tourism and what is rural. However, if a definition of tourism as a whole is applied to the specific context of the countryside, then the scope of rural tourism becomes much broader.

One problem that immediately emerges is that tourism itself is difficult to define. It is a diverse, social activity involving millions of individuals who travel either internationally or within their own country, participating in a multitude of activities. Furthermore, tourism is supported by a vast, yet fragmented, industry which provides tourists with transport, accommodation, attractions, refreshment facilities, information services, souvenirs and so on. In other words, tourism is 'a multidimensional, multifaceted activity, which touches many lives and many different economic activities' (Cooper *et al.* 1993). Numerous attempts have been made to define tourism (Nash 1981; Mathieson and Wall 1982; Smith 1989) and to classify tourists (Cohen 1972, 1974; Lowyck *et al.* 1992; Plog 1977; Smith 1989) but, generally, definitions of tourism fall into two groups or categories, reflecting, on the one hand, tourism as a social activity and, on the other hand, tourism as an economic activity or industry. These two categories have been described (Burkhart and Medlik 1981: 41–43) as *conceptual* definitions, which are concerned with the nature or meaning of tourism as a social activity, and *technical* definitions, which attempt to identify different types of tourist and different tourism activities, normally for statistical or legislative purposes.

At the heart of conceptual definitions lies the individual as a tourist and Nash (1981), for example, defines tourism simply as the activity undertaken by a 'person at leisure who also travels'. Other definitions emphasise motivational aspects, tourism being defined in terms of a form of escape or change from normal day to day life and work, involving journeys to and stays at sites away from the usual places of residence or work (see Urry 1990a: 2–3) but, typically, conceptual definitions highlight the meaning and purpose of tourism to those who participate in it. In this context, rural tourism may be defined as a state of mind whereby tourists are actively seeking a leisure experience in a rural environment.

Conversely, technical definitions of tourism represent, in effect, a set of criteria by which to identify and measure tourism and, according to Murphy (1985: 5), one of the most widely recognised definitions is the one which was produced by the United Nations Conference on Travel and Tourism in 1963 and later adopted by the International Union of Official Travel Organisations (IOUTO), the precursor to the World Tourism Organisation (WTO). It states that a visitor is:

> any person visiting a country other than that in which he [sic] has his usual place of residence, for any reason other than following an occupation remunerated from within the country visited,

a visitor being either a tourist, who stays overnight, or an excursionist on a day visit. However, a major drawback of this definition is that it excludes domestic tourism which, in most countries, represents the larger proportion of rural tourism and, therefore, a more appropriate technical definition is that suggested by the Tourism Society in Britain:

> Tourism is the temporary short-term movement of people to destinations outside the places where they normally live and work, and activities during their stay at these destinations; it includes movement for all purposes, as well as day visits or excursions.

One implication of this statement is that tourism encompasses many more purposes and activities than is traditionally assumed. In other words, it not only includes all varieties of holidays but also business trips, leisure activities, sports, and a range of other purposes not normally associated with tourism. The two main characteristics of tourism are that it involves travel away from home or the workplace and short-term stays at destinations (though not necessarily including an overnight stay) and, therefore, the list of activities that can be classified as tourism is virtually endless. For simplicity, however, four distinct categories can be identified:

- Holidays, including main holidays, second and third holidays, short breaks and day trips.
- Business, excluding permanent residence or remuneration in the destination.
- Visiting friends and relatives.
- Other, including travel for education, sport, health and religion.

If these four categories are applied to tourism in the countryside in particular, it becomes evident that rural tourism, from an activity point of view, is a much broader concept than might be imagined. Indeed, in 1986 the Commission of the European Communities defined rural tourism as including 'not only farm tourism or agritourism . . . but all tourist activities in rural areas'. Little is to be gained from attempting to identify all of these tourist activities; however, the scope of rural tourism is clearly indicated in a list suggested by the Council of Europe (Table 1.1).

It is also important to stress that a number of different tourism products or types of tourism development fall under the heading of rural tourism.

Table 1.1 Range of tourist leisure activities in the countryside

1. **Touring**
   - hiking (footpaths, fitness trails, nature parks);
   - horse riding;
   - touring in gypsy caravans, wagons;
   - motorised touring (trail riding, all-terrain vehicles, motoring);
   - cycling;
   - donkey riding;
   - cross-country skiing.
2. **Water-related activities**
   - fishing;
   - swimming;
   - river tourism (Houseboats, narrow boats, barges);
   - canoeing and rafting;
   - windsurfing;
   - speedboat racing;
   - sailing;
   - facilities of the 'aqualand' type.
3. **Aerial activities**
   - light aircraft;
   - hang-gliding and microlight aircraft;
   - hot air balloons.
4. **Activities on dry land**
   - tennis;
   - golf.
5. **Sporting activities**
   - pot-holing;
   - rock climbing.
6. **Discovery-type activities**
   - local industrial, agricultural or craft enterprises.
7. **Cultural activities**
   - archaeology;
   - restoration sites;
   - courses in crafts;
   - artistic expression workshops;
   - folk groups;
   - cultural, gastronomic and other routes.
8. **Health-related activities**
   - fitness training;
   - health resorts.

Source: Thibal 1988

However, they do not necessarily equate with it. For example, farm tourism refers to 'all forms of tourism that are directly connected with a farm' (Jansen-Verbeke and Nijmegen 1990) and includes staying on a farm, either in rooms or camping, educational visits, meals, recreational activities, and the sale of farm produce or handicrafts. Other terms describing forms of tourism in rural areas are:

- *Agritourism* – this is often used to describe all tourism activities in rural areas (although, strictly, it means tourism on the land) and, in some countries, refers to what is defined here as rural tourism. However, agritourism, more frequently, comprises those tourism products which are 'directly connected with the agrarian environment, agrarian products or agrarian stays' (Jansen-Verbeke and Nijmegen 1990). In other words, agritourism is tourism linked to agriculture; farm-based tourism is, therefore, one element of agritourism, but agritourism is a broader concept which also covers festivals, museums, craft shows and other cultural events and attractions.
- *Green tourism* – although in some countries the term 'green tourism' refers specifically to tourism in the countryside (i.e. tourism in green areas), it is more commonly used to describe forms of tourism that are considered to be more environmentally friendly than traditional, mass tourism. Variously called 'alternative', 'responsible', 'soft', 'good' (Wood and House 1991) or 'new' (Poon 1993) tourism, green tourism is an approach to tourism development which seeks to develop a symbiotic relationship (Budowski 1976) with the physical and social environment on which it depends. In other words, increasing concern about the harmful effects of mass tourism has led to calls for more sustainable forms of tourism development. Such an approach is, of course, of particular relevance to rural tourism given the environmental fragility of many rural areas, and it is discussed at greater length in Chapter 2.
- *Ecotourism* – this is a form of tourism development which 'offers unique opportunities for integrating rural development, tourism, resource management, and protected area management in many sites around the world' (Hvenegaard 1994). More specifically, it is a form of nature tourism (tourism to natural, unspoilt areas) which actively promotes environmental conservation, is directly beneficial to local societies and cultures, and which provides tourists with a positive, educative experience. It is, in effect, a form of alternative, sustainable tourism (Cater and Lowman 1994: 3), but one which, implicitly, depends on a rural environment. Hence, ecotourism is a subset of rural tourism, but not all rural tourism is necessarily ecotourism.

The following case study, describing the development of 'agritourism' in Cyprus, is an example of one form of tourism development in rural areas.

Case study 1: The development of agritourism in Cyprus.

In 1960, when Cyprus gained its independence from Britain, its tourism industry was virtually non-existent. Other than a number of small-scale, family run businesses located in the hill resorts in the Troodos mountains there were virtually no tourism facilities and, in that year, the island attracted just 25,700 tourists. By 1990, after 30 years of rapid growth in its tourism industry, Cyprus had become one of the major Mediterranean holiday destinations with over 1.5 million international visitors; by 1994, that figure had passed the 2 million mark.

Even more remarkable is the fact that the Cyprus tourism industry has had to be developed twice. Many of the original facilities, resorts and attractions were located in the north of the island around the principal resorts of Famagusta and Kyrenia (see Figure 1.1). Following the Turkish invasion and occupation in 1974, the Cypriot government had to rebuild the tourism industry virtually from scratch. A new airport was constructed at Larnaca, new resorts were developed at Paphos, Limassol, Paralimni and Ayia Napa and, by 1990, Cyprus had a thriving tourism industry based upon the traditional sun, sea and sand package holiday.

One notable feature of the growth of tourism in Cyprus is that virtually all new developments have been in coastal areas. This is has resulted in a rapid growth in accommodation facilities in the coastal resorts, particularly since 1985, whilst the hill resorts, once the mainstay of the island's fledgling tourism industry, have been largely ignored (Table 1.2). Indeed, there were *fewer* registered bed spaces in the hill resorts in 1990 than in 1960, when just over 1700 bed spaces

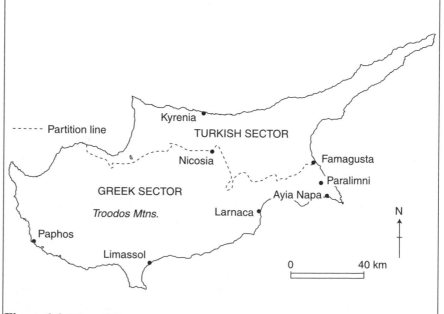

Figure 1.1 Map of Cyprus †

Table 1.2 Accomodation capacity in Cyprus, 1985–1990 ('000 beds)

	1985	1986	1987	1988	1989	1990
Hotels						
Nicosia	2.0	2.1	2.1	2.1	2.1	2.1
Limassol	4.7	5.2	6.1	6.2	6.8	7.5
Larnaka	3.2	3.6	3.6	3.8	4.0	4.6
Ayia Napa	3.4	3.5	3.8	4.4	5.1	5.4
Paralimni	1.1	1.2	1.8	1.8	2.0	2.9
Paphos	2.6	2.8	3.0	3.9	4.8	5.9
Hill Resorts	1.1	1.2	1.1	1.2	1.3	1.2
Total	**18.2**	**19.6**	**21.6**	**23.3**	**26.1**	**29.5**
Appartments						
Nicosia	0.1	0.1	0.1	0.1	0.1	0.1
Limassol	2.6	3.0	3.1	3.5	3.5	3.5
Larnaka	3.0	3.1	3.1	3.4	3.6	3.2
Ayia Napa	2.8	3.3	4.1	4.7	5.6	5.7
Paralimni	1.3	1.6	2.3	2.6	3.4	5.0
Paphos	1.0	1.1	1.1	1.3	1.4	1.8
Hill Resorts	–	–	–	–	–	–
Total	**10.8**	**12.3**	**14.1**	**15.6**	**17.6**	**19.1**

Source: EIU 1992

represented almost 45 per cent of Cyprus' total accommodation capacity (Andronikou 1987).

This concentration of tourism development inevitably meant that the coastal areas benefited most from tourism generated income (1992 receipts from tourism amounted to about US$1.5 billion) and infrastructural improvements, whilst the hinterland, described as 'all areas apart from the coastal zone and urban centres' (CTO undated) suffered from social and economic decline.

In order to spread the benefits of tourism inland and to reverse the decline in rural communities, the CTO has been promoting the development of agritourism since the early 1990s. Based upon the existing infrastructure and respecting the physical and cultural characteristics of the hinterland, the overall purpose is to diversify the Cyprus tourism product, bringing extra income to rural villages and, indirectly, restraining the depopulation of the countryside. The CTO plans to attract tourists who are interested in 'alternative' holidays, offering opportunities for hiking, bird-watching, visiting historical or archaeological sites or learning local skills and traditions. Visitors will stay in converted local buildings and eat at local restaurants and tavernas, thereby gaining an experience of traditional life in a rural Cypriot community.

Funding has been made available to provide low interest loans for the restoration and development of buildings into accommodation facilities, tavernas or craft shops, and to develop appropriate infrastructure and facilities. Furthermore, it is hoped that each village participating in the scheme will develop various attractions based upon local culture, emphasising the traditionally rural nature of the tourism experience.

Some sixteen villages are participating in the scheme and are still at the developmental stage.

However, a similar scheme, known as the Laona Project, was implemented in 1989 in the Laona region on the western tip of the island. Based on an initiative of Friends of the Earth Cyprus, the project was designed to promote small-scale eco-tourism on the Akamas Peninsula, one of the last remaining undeveloped areas of Cyprus and home to the nesting grounds of the loggerhead and green turtle (see Yiordamli 1995). Supported by EU and private funding, the project was involved in the restoration of 26 buildings in five separate villages, including accommodation units, tavernas and a visitor centre which attracted over 11,000 visitors in 1994.

Over its five year life, the original Laona Project achieved most of its objectives and, managed by the Foundation for the Revival of Laona, it now forms part of the broader Blue Plan for the development of the Akamas Peninsula. The Blue Plan aims to implement the principles of sustainable rural tourism in the region, designating the peninsula as a national park and concentrating all developments within the existing villages. It is hoped that, by 2010, the area will attract 10,000 tourists a year (Ioannides 1995), bringing significant employment opportunities and income to one of the poorest parts of Cyprus. However, locally the plan is considered to represent an undue restriction on development and has attracted much opposition amongst local people who have witnessed the rapid development and increasing wealth in other parts of Cyprus. Thus, the viability of agritourism development in a traditional sun, sea and sand holiday destination such as Cyprus remains to be seen.

From this brief analysis in this section (see Gilbert 1990 for a more detailed discussion of tourism definitions), it is evident that people visit the countryside as tourists for diverse reasons, and participate in a large variety of activities and pursuits once they are there. Furthermore, rural tourism also encompasses a number of specialist forms of tourism linked to particular characteristics of the rural environment and rural tourism can be defined both technically (according to activities, destinations and other statistical measurements) and conceptually (in terms of the meaning of the countryside as a tourism destination). Thus, the scope of rural tourism is, to a great extent, limited only by the location in which it occurs. The next task, therefore, is to define what we mean by 'countryside'.

WHAT IS 'COUNTRYSIDE'?

In its report *What Future for Our Countryside?*, The Organisation for Economic Co-operation and Development (OECD) states:

> Rural areas comprise the people, land and other resources, in the open country and small settlements outside the immediate economic

influence of major urban centres. Rural is a territorial or spatial concept. It is not restricted to any particular use of land, degree of economic health, or economic sector.

(OECD 1993: 11)

Thus, the countryside can be defined simply as those areas which lie
beyond major towns and cities and which are, therefore, rural, as opposed
to urban, in character. On the basis that rural areas are non-urban, this definition is necessarily broad; it includes a number of features, such as
forests, reservoirs, canals, beaches and agricultural land, which might not
be normally considered as rural tourism destinations.

However, when the fact that rural areas make up about 90 per cent of the
territory of OECD member countries is taken into account, this also
appears to be an overly simplistic definition. That is, such is the diversity
of lands forms, land usages, social structures and cultures in rural areas
that some clarification of the meaning of rural, as opposed to urban, is
required. Moreover, within the context of tourism, not all rural areas are
equally suitable or viable for tourism development and it is a useful exercise, therefore, to link particular features of rural areas with their potential
for tourism.

Lane (1994a) suggests three main characteristics which clearly identify
areas as rural:

● population density and size of settlement;
● land use and economy;
● traditional social structures.

Population density/settlement size

If rural areas are considered primarily to be 'non-urban' then, by definition,
they are characterised by low population densities and relatively small settlements. Of course, population density varies enormously between regions
and countries, as do the criteria by which towns and villages are judged to
be either urban or rural. Throughout the world, different countries employ
different population levels to delineate between urban and rural areas
(Table 1.3), whilst, even within Europe, such is the variety of geographical,

Table 1.3 National criteria for 'rural' settlements

Australia	Population clusters of less than 1000 people, excluding certain areas, e.g. holiday resorts.
Austria	Parishes of less than 5000 people.
Canada	Places of less than 1000 people, with a population density of less than 400 per square km.
Denmark (and Norway)	Agglomerations of less than 200 inhabitants.
France	Towns containing an agglomeration of fewer than 2000 people living in contiguous houses, or with not more than 200 metres between the houses.
Portugal	Towns of fewer than 10,000 people.

Source: Lane 1994a

demographic and socio-economic factors that there is no agreed population threshold. In the UK, for example, there is no recognised or official population size at which a rural settlement becomes urban, although towns and villages with less than 10,000 inhabitants are considered to be rural (ETB 1988). Italy and Spain employ the same figure, whereas 'the distinction between aggregate urban areas and aggregate rural areas in Ireland is set at 100 inhabitants' (Hoggart *et al.* 1995: 22).

However, in the context of tourism, it is not the figures themselves that are of importance, although they do indicate the difficulty in achieving internationally accepted criteria of rurality. Rather, it is the comparison between the tourist's home (and usually urban) environment and the characteristics of the destination that mark it as rural. A major attraction of rural areas for tourists is the sense of space and the lack of urban development, and perceptions of these will undoubtedly vary according to where tourists live and their own experience (Harrison 1991). As a rule of thumb, however, it could be argued that the more sparsely populated an area is, the more attractive it will be to tourists.

Land use and economy

A variety of demands are placed upon the countryside, primarily agriculture, forestry and the extraction of natural resources. These may all be thought of as traditional, non-urban and non-industrial land uses, despite the increasingly industrial nature of farming in many countries, and they represent the second important element of the overall picture of the countryside. In other words, rural areas may be defined as those with economies based upon traditional agrarian or forestry industries.

However, the rural/urban dichotomy in the context of economic activity is becoming less distinct, particularly in the developed world. The continuing decline in the relative importance of the agricultural sector and the growth of the post-industrial, service sector has led to many new industries, including tourism, being developed in rural areas. As a result, the traditional view of the countryside and rural economic activity is having to adapt to take into account this 'reconstruction' of the countryside (Marsden *et al.* 1993)

The relevance of this to tourism is that it is not only the character of rural land use and economic activity but also its intensity and diversity that determines the potential for rural tourism development. On the one hand, intensively farmed areas or prosperous and diverse rural economies will have less need to develop tourism and may be less attractive to tourists. On the other hand, economically marginal areas which depend on traditional, small-scale agrarian industries will have a greater need for economic diversification and may be more attractive to tourists.

Traditional social structures

Of all the perceptions of rurality, perhaps the most widely held, particularly amongst urban residents, is that the countryside retains the traditional social structures and values that have been lost in modern, urban society. The extent to which this is a romantic idyll of rural life as opposed to an objective assessment of rural society remains a subject of both debate and research (Halfacree 1995), but there is little doubt that rural societies possess a variety of characteristics which, collectively, identify them as being more traditional than modern, urban societies. Of course, all societies, urban or rural, are dynamic and in a constant state of change and development, whilst not all rural societies demonstrate what may be described as traditional attributes. Nevertheless, social structures in the countryside may be typified by a variety of characteristics including a sense of community, simple economies, local rather than cosmopolitan cultures and a way of life that is somehow slower, less materialistic and more complete than in urban societies.

The traditional nature of rural societies has a number of implications for the development of tourism. Undoubtedly, tourists are motivated by the desire to see or experience different, traditional lifestyles as part of the ever-increasing interest in heritage. Furthermore, tourism, if carefully managed, can contribute to the maintenance of these traditional social and cultural structures (hence, the frequent association of rural tourism with eco-tourism or sustainable tourism). Conversely, tourism can easily undermine social structures and threaten the stability of rural societies and cultures, destroying the very thing that attracts tourists in the first place. Thus, there is a need for careful planning and management of tourism to maintain the character and well-being of rural societies.

A further problem encountered when trying to define 'countryside' is that there is no sharp dividing line between urban areas and rural areas. Some areas are essentially rural but display a number of urban characteristics, whereas other areas are primarily urban but convey a sense of rurality. In other words, there is a kind of scale of rurality, a 'rural–urban continuum' (Lane 1994a), along which different areas can be located. Typically, areas with few rural characteristics are to be found on the urban fringe or in 'green belts', whereas more remote, peripheral areas (OECD 1993: 32) conform more closely to the three characteristics of rurality described above.

These different types of countryside and their use as a resource for rural tourism are explored in greater detail in the next chapter. To return to the theme of this section, however, it is evident that the countryside is, indeed, best defined as those areas which lie beyond larger towns and cities and which, to varying degrees, display the characteristics of rurality described here. The concept of countryside, therefore, is much broader than might be initially apparent and, furthermore, it introduces the notion that rural tourism is not restricted to industrialised, Western nations. Although much of the rural tourism literature is concerned with Europe or North America, many parts of the developing world also conform to our definition of rurality. The hills of northern Thailand, the game reserves of East Africa or the Mayan villages of Central America, all popular tourism destinations, are as equally rural as other areas more normally considered to be countryside.

Moreover, within the context of tourism development, they also face the same challenges and problems. Therefore, although this book is primarily concerned with rural tourism in the more conventional sense, many of the issues are of broader relevance, including the extent to which the countryside has a deeper, cultural significance.

THE CULTURAL SIGNIFICANCE OF THE COUNTRYSIDE

For many visitors, in particular those who normally live and work in an urban environment, the countryside can be more than simply a convenient location in which to participate in certain activities. That is not to say that visitors are not attracted by the physical attributes of rural areas, for many forms of rural tourism depend on the rural environment: mountaineers need mountains, fishermen require lakes and rivers, farm holidays require farms. However, the attraction of the countryside as a tourist destination goes beyond both its tangible, visible characteristics and its inherent qualities, such as open space, fresh air, or peace and quiet. It also *represents* something to visitors. In other words, rural areas can be defined, as discussed above, not only by locational and societal characteristics, but also as an abstract concept, a social construction 'used by people in everyday talk' (Halfacree 1993).

Typically, this concept of the countryside possessing symbolic significance is accepted to be a relatively recent phenomenon resulting from the industrialisation and urbanisation of society, although pastoral images of the countryside originate in ancient times (Short 1991: 29). As modern (urban) life has become faster, more stressful and less 'authentic', the countryside has increasingly come to be seen as a rural utopia, a green and pleasant land (Newby 1985) where people can escape from the present into a nostalgic past. In effect, the countryside has achieved almost mythical status as a simpler, better place than the city, where life is slower, more natural and more meaningful.

Nowhere has this rural myth become more ingrained in national culture than in England (Lowenthal and Prince 1965), where the countryside and all it represents is firmly embedded in the country's heritage (Wright 1985) yet, 'in most countries the countryside has become the embodiment of the nation . . . a combination of nature and culture which best represents the nation-state' (Short 1991: 35). Thus, in most countries, rural areas have a deeper, cultural significance which may, to a greater or lesser extent, influence social practices in general and tourism in particular. It has been argued, for example, that both rural tourists and the policies of those organisations entrusted with the planning and management of recreation in rural areas in England are guided by a countryside 'aesthetic' (Harrison 1991) based on a romantic, pre-industrial idyll of rural England, a 'chocolate box' countryside of meadows, villages and country lanes. For example, the Countryside Commission, the principal organisation concerned with conservation and the promotion of recreation in the English countryside, bases many of its policies on the understanding that the English have 'a deep love for, and response to, the countryside' (Countryside Commission 1987a). Conversely, the countryside as a tourist destination in the United States is primarily viewed as preserved 'wilderness' areas in the national parks of the West and Far West of the country (Shaw and Williams 1994: 227).

Importantly, countryside as a social construction is also relevant in an international dimension. Although much of the literature is concerned with urban, or even rural, residents' perceptions of their own countryside, the popularity of many international destinations is also largely dependent on the cultural significance attached to those destinations by tourists. In other words, just as many urban residents consider rural areas in their own country to be a 'refuge from modernity' (Short 1991: 34), so too may tourists perceive other countries, particularly in the developing world, to be more traditional than their own. The tourism industry, through its brochures and advertising, reinforces popularly held images of destinations (Silver 1993), and many countries are sold to tourists on the basis of an 'authentic' rurality which satisfies the expectations of visitors but which may bear little relation to reality.

A deeper examination of the links between tourism and authenticity are beyond the scope of this book (see, for example, Cohen 1988; MacCannell 1989; Sharpley 1994). Nevertheless, the notion that the countryside can be defined both locationally, in opposition to urban areas, and as a social construction is of fundamental importance to the study of rural tourism and is of relevance to many issues considered in later chapters.

RURAL TOURISM: MARKET SECTOR OR DEVELOPMENT PHILOSOPHY?

In an attempt to develop a broad understanding of the breadth and scope of rural tourism, the previous sections have highlighted and discussed a number of points within two specific contexts, namely:

- the activities and forms of tourism that are encompassed by rural tourism;
- the environment in which rural tourism is located.

In order to further clarify what is meant by the term 'rural tourism', it is also necessary to consider rural tourism within the broader picture of all tourism. We must ask, in particular, whether rural tourism is simply one sector of the overall market for tourism or whether it is a means of describing a particular approach to the development of tourism in rural areas.

At first sight, it is certainly justifiable to consider rural tourism as a market sector. Frequently described as a form of 'special interest' tourism (as opposed to the mass, package holiday market), rural tourism is just one of many different sectors that, together, comprise the overall tourism market. In other words, rural tourism is one of a range of tourism 'products' available to potential tourists and, in effect, it competes with other market sectors, such as city tourism, the traditional sun-sea-sand market or cruising, for a share of all tourism. Importantly, tourism itself is a growth market. Since 1970, worldwide international arrivals and international receipts have grown at an average annual rate of 5.1 per cent and 12.8 per cent respectively (see Table 1.4); domestic tourism is estimated to represent about ten times the value and volume of international tourism and overall, according to the World Travel and Tourism Council, world tourism grew by a remarkable 260 per cent between 1970 and 1990 and is now worth over $3 trillion (WTTC 1994).

In view of the dominance of domestic tourism in worldwide tourism figures and the increasing popularity of forms of tourism which comprise rural tourism, such as ecotourism and nature tourism, rural tourism therefore represents a large and important sector of the overall tourism market.

However, given the somewhat ambiguous nature of rural tourism and the difficulty in delineating between rural and other forms of tourism (for example, some types of beach holidays could be included under the rural tourism heading, whilst many tourism activities that occur in rural areas may be categorised under other tourism headings), accurately quantifying it in terms of visits, overnight stays or spending would be a difficult, if not impossible, task. Therefore, it is logical to conclude that a more conceptual approach is needed to separate rural from other forms of tourism.

It has been suggested rural tourism can be defined according to its relationship with its environment (Lane 1994a). That is, for tourism to be described as rural, then, logically, it should mirror those characteristics which signify an area as rural, namely, small settlements, low population densities, agrarian-based economies and traditional social structures. Thus, rural tourism should be developed in a manner which emphasises and reflects the rural environment; it should be rural in scale and char-

Table 1.4 International arrivals and receipts, 1970–94

Year	Arrivals ('000)	Receipts (US$ million)
1970	159,700	17,900
1980	284,300	103,100
1981	286,700	105,200
1982	286,600	98,500
1983	289,900	101,000
1984	317,100	111,000
1985	327,600	116,100
1986	338,600	140,600
1987	364,800	172,500
1988	399,700	199,500
1989	429,000	215,600
1990	455,500	261,000
1991	463,200	267,500
1992	502,900	304,000
1993	512,900	305,800
1994	528,400	321,500

Source: WTO (1995)

acter and building upon the features and attributes of its surroundings, it should utilise existing buildings and facilities, involve the local community and it should be limited by an area's physical, social and cultural capacity to absorb tourism.

Of course, this describes an ideal version of rural tourism and one which is rarely to be found. Nevertheless, it is a version of tourism which is sought by many tourism planners and authorities (Table 1.5), and one which reflects the broader principles of sustainable tourism. Therefore, it is not surprising that rural tourism is frequently equated with sustainable tourism, ecotourism, alternative tourism and other types of small-scale, low impact tourism development.

In reality, many forms of tourism which occur in rural areas do not conform to these guidelines and, therefore, to describe rural tourism as a particular approach or philosophy of tourism develop-ment is to limit artificially the scope of the subject. However, it does draw attention to broader arguments regarding the extent to which rural areas should be conserved or developed (Fairbrother 1972) and to the fact that a special feature of the countryside is its rurality; if rural tourism relies on that rurality, 'if rurality in its many manifes-tations is a unique selling point, then great care must be taken to maintain rurality' (Lane 1994a).

Table 1.5 Principles for tourism in the countryside

Enjoyment	The promotion of tourist enjoyment of the countryside should be primarily aimed at those activities which draw on the character of the countryside itself, its beauty, culture, history and wildlife.
Development	Tourism development in the countryside should assist the purposes of conservation and recreation. It can, for example, bring new uses to historic houses, supplement usage and incomes to farms, aid the reclamation of derelict land and open up new opportunities for access to the countryside.
Design	The planning, siting and management of new tourism developments should be in keeping with the landscape and wherever possible should seek to enhance it.
Rural economy	Investment in tourism should support the rural economy, but should seek a wider geographical spread and more off peak visiting both to avoid congestion and damage to the resource through erosion and over use, and to spread the economic and other benefits.
Conservation	Those who benefit from tourism in the countryside should contribute to the conservation and enhancement of its most valuable asset, the countryside, through political and practical support for conservation and recreational policies and programmes.
Marketing	Publicity, information and marketing initiatives of the tourism industry should endeavour to deepen people's understanding of and concern for the countryside leading to a fuller appreciation and enjoyment.

Source: English Tourist Board/Countryside Commission 1989

CONCLUSION

In attempting to answer the question 'what is rural tourism?', this chapter has demonstrated that rural tourism, both as an identifiable type of tourism and as a subject of academic study, is a much broader concept than might initially be imagined. It comprises a whole host of activities and pursuits, some of which may be considered more traditionally rural than others, and it occurs in an enormous variety of different environments which, again, may be considered more or less rural.

It would appear, therefore, that the simplest way to define rural tourism is, indeed, tourism that occurs in rural areas. However, as is evident from the points discussed in this chapter, it is a definition which requires clarification. Thus, for the purposes of this book:

- 'Rural' describes all areas, both land and water, that lie beyond towns and cities which, in national or regional contexts, may be described as major urban centres.
- 'Tourism' includes long and short holidays, day visits, and both domestic and international travel. It includes all activities that may be categorised as recreation.
- 'Rural tourism' may be defined both conceptually, as a state of mind, and technically, according to activities, destinations and other measurable, tangible characteristics.
- 'Rurality' refers both to the identifiable characteristics of rural areas and the cultural meaning attached to rural areas and is of fundamental importance to the demand for, and supply of, rural tourism.

Above all, rural tourism is a form of economic activity which depends upon, and exploits, the countryside. Therefore, the next chapter considers the implications of the use of the countryside as a resource for tourism development.

QUESTIONS

1. Why is it difficult to define rural tourism?
2. What is 'countryside'?
3. Compare the different types of tourism that may collectively be described as rural tourism.
4. To what extent is the countryside a cultural myth as opposed to a physical reality?

FURTHER READING

Bunce, M. (1994) *The Countryside Ideal: Anglo-American Images of Landscape*, London: Routledge.

Hunter, C. and Green, H. (1995) *Tourism and the Environment: A Sustainable Relationship?*, London: Routledge.

OECD (1994) *Tourism Policy and International Tourism in OECD Countries 1991–1992* (Special Feature: Tourism Strategies and Rural Development), Paris: OECD.

Sharpley, R. (1996) *Tourism and Leisure in the Countryside*, 2nd Edition, Huntingdon: Elm Publications.

Thibal, S. (1988) *Rural Tourism in Europe*, Strasbourg: Council of Europe.

2 The countryside: a resource for tourism

INTRODUCTION

Rural tourism is, by definition, tourism which occurs in rural areas. Moreover, although the distinction between rural and non-rural areas is not always clear, it is generally held that 'for many urban dwellers, it is the rural ambience and the countryside experience which are the main considerations' (Pigram 1993: 161) when participating in rural tourism. Thus, the countryside, in both the physical and cultural sense of the word, is a resource for tourism. It is a resource which attracts tourists, a resource which is exploited by the tourism industry for financial gain and, by implication, a resource upon which both tourists and the tourism industry depend. At the same time, in many areas of both the developing and industrialised worlds, tourism is increasingly seen as a valid and important means of sustaining and diversifying rural economies and societies; in the face of the declining role of agriculture and the increasing marginalisation of many rural areas, tourism has become the new 'cash crop' in the countryside. Thus, a two-way relationship exists between rural tourism and the resource upon which it depends.

However, this relationship is not so simple as might immediately be apparent. Tourism and agriculture are not the only demands placed on the countryside and a variety of other uses and demands compete for a share of the resource. Nor is the countryside in endless supply. Some demands, such as housing development, 'use up' the countryside, diminishing its overall supply. For example, in England it has been estimated that, between 1945 and 1990, a total of 705,000 hectares of countryside was lost to urbanisation. This is the equivalent of a rural area the size of Greater London being urbanised every decade (CPRE 1992). Moreover, many parts of the countryside are fragile and susceptible to damage from a large number of uses, including tourism. Throughout the industrialised world, for example, the most common means of visiting the countryside is by car and tangible evidence has been found of the destructive effects of vehicle emissions on rural areas, particularly forests (Whitelegg 1993). Similarly, many national parks around the world are in danger of being 'loved to death' by the ever increasing numbers of visitors (FNNPE 1993).

The purpose of this chapter, therefore, is to examine the countryside as a resource for tourism. It introduces the range of different demands placed upon the countryside and examines, in particular, the link between agricultural and rural development policies and the promotion of tourism. The benefits and impacts of tourism on the countryside are also considered and three themes are implicit throughout the chapter:

● The countryside is a multi-purpose resource which supports a variety of demands and uses, including tourism.
● The countryside is a finite, fragile resource.
● Effective, proactive planning and management is necessary to minimise potential conflicts and to ensure the sustainable use of the rural resource.

THE COUNTRYSIDE: A MULTI-PURPOSE RESOURCE

Throughout history, agriculture and forestry have been the dominant land uses in rural areas. They have shaped the landscape, they have traditionally provided the main source of income and employment in the countryside and, perhaps inevitably, they have also directly influenced the structure and culture of rural societies. In most industrialised nations, up to 80 per cent of rural land is still farmed or forested (see, for example, Hoggart *et al.* 1995 for a detailed examination of land use in rural Europe) although, significantly, the contribution of agriculture and forestry to income and employment in rural areas has gradually diminished during the twentieth century, as has their relative contribution to GDP in most countries. One indication of this trend has been the diversification of rural economies and the emergence of 'pluriactivity' amongst farming communities. It has been found, for example, that just 17 per cent of European farm households earn all their income directly from agriculture whilst, at the other end of the scale, over 40 per cent derive less than one third of their income from agriculture (Fuller 1990). One new source of income for farmers is, of course, tourism.

Importantly, however, it is not only the role of agriculture and forestry that has changed. Economic, social and technological transformations and developments over the last two centuries have resulted in new, diverse demands on rural areas, demands which have increasingly challenged the traditional influence of agriculture and forestry on rural life and land use in the countryside. Equally, the characteristics of different demands and uses have also changed; for example, traditional farming techniques have been replaced by intensive, large-scale agribusiness, whilst rural tourism itself has undergone a fundamental transformation in both volume and scope during the last fifty years or so. Together, these changes have been a source of increasing conflict and concern, particularly within the context of increasing environmental awareness (see Clark *et al.* 1994).

In short, the countryside has become a multi-purpose resource supporting a variety of different demands and uses. At the same time, attitudes towards the countryside have expanded as more is expected of it as a resource, whether as a new business location, as a place to live, or as temporary escape from modern, urban life (Waters 1994). Tourism, therefore, is just one of many demands on the countryside and, as Pigram (1993: 161) suggests, the multi-purpose character of the countryside represents both an opportunity and a constraint to tourism development. On the one hand, tourism can be viewed as a valid and valuable form of land use which, if carefully planned and managed, complements other uses and contributes to the economic and social well-being of rural areas; on the other hand, it may be considered that other, more traditional forms of economic exploitation of the land, including farming, mineral extraction and housing, should take precedence over its recreational potential. Thus, it is perhaps inevitable that, given the finite supply of countryside, conflicts occur between different demands on the rural resource base. It is important, therefore, to identify the primary uses with which tourism shares the countryside.

Farming and agriculture

The influence of farming and agriculture on the countryside cannot be overstated. Farming has always been the dominant land use in rural areas and, prior to the rapid industrialisation and urbanisation of Western societies from around 1800 onwards, virtually all social life was agrarian in character. Farming and agriculture has also been largely responsible for shaping rural landscapes and, throughout much of the latter half of the twentieth century, this influential role has been reinforced in many countries by government policies designed to support food production. These policies, in turn, have led to the introduction of intensive farming methods, particularly in northern Europe and North America, which, since the 1950s, have resulted in a rapid and fundamental transformation of the landscape in many rural areas. Large areas of previously uncultivated land have fallen under the plough, hedgerows, woods and walls have been removed to create 'prairie' fields, wetlands have been drained, and the widespread use of chemical fertilisers and pesticides, whilst undoubtedly increasing yields, have had a potentially destructive effect on wildlife.

Inevitably, this second 'agricultural revolution' has attracted fierce criticism (see Carson 1965; Shoard 1980) although, in recent years, farmers have been encouraged to adopt more traditional, environmentally benign methods which maintain the landscape and wildlife habitats. In England, the introduction of schemes such as Environmentally Sensitive Areas (ESAs) and Countryside Stewardship (Countryside Commission 1991a) have emphasised the importance of conserving the countryside, but are also significant inasmuch as they recognise the importance of the countryside as a resource for tourism. Indeed, as a result of the Agriculture Act 1986, the Ministry of Agriculture, Fisheries and Food (MAFF) has had a legal duty to maintain a balance between an efficient farming industry, the social and economic needs of rural communities, conservation of the natural beauty of the countryside and, importantly, the promotion of the enjoyment of the countryside by the public.

The relationship between agricultural policies and the promotion of tourism is explored in greater detail later in this chapter. However, in terms of land use, farming and agriculture have traditionally superseded the needs of visitors. Access both to and within the countryside has been lost (Shoard 1987), the proprietorial rights of landowners have, in the past, dominated other demands on the resource, and studies in Canada and Europe have shown that the availability of recreational opportunities in the countryside have been inversely proportional to the intensity of land use, in particular farming (Millward 1992; 1993). Thus, the more recent trends towards pluriactivity in farming and agriculture and policies which encourage the provision of access for visitors indicate that tourism and farming are becoming less mutually exclusive demands on the countryside.

Forestry

Along with farming and agriculture, forestry has also long been a dominant land use in rural areas. Throughout Europe, the great majority of the countryside is dominated by either agriculture or forestry and, although the proportions vary by country, roughly a quarter of all rural space is, on average, utilised for forestry (Table 2.1). The UK has one of the lowest proportions of forested land in Europe although, since the establishment of the Forestry Commission in 1919, the British forest area has increased from 5 to 10 per cent of the country's land surface area.

The primary purpose of forestry is, of course, the production of wood and wood products. However, forests are also an integral feature of rural landscapes, they are an important ecological resource and, globally, they play a vital environmental role. This was formally recognised by the 1992 Earth Summit in Rio de Janeiro, which adopted a set of principles to guide the sustainable and multiple use of the world's forests (Forestry Commission 1993).

One such use of forests is recreation and tourism. Forests play host to a variety of formal (managed) and informal activities, ranging from walking and camping to orienteering and rally driving. In the UK, the recreational

Table 2.1 Rural land use in Europe (per cent)

Country	Farmland	Forests	Water	Other
Belgium	45.0	20.2	0.9	33.9
Denmark	65.2	11.4	1.6	21.7
France	55.7	26.9	1.1	16.3
Germany	47.8	29.6	1.8	20.8
Greece	35.8	43.6	2.4	*
Ireland	81.0	4.7	2.0	12.3
Italy	57.1	21.0	2.4	19.4
Luxembourg	48.7	34.3	0.4	16.6
Netherlands	48.4	7.9	9.1	24.0
Portugal	49.3	32.2	0.5	18.1
Spain	53.7	24.8	1.1	20.4
UK	73.7	9.4	1.3	15.5

* No figure available
Source: Eurostat (1992) – adapted

potential of forests was formally recognised as early as 1936 when the first Forest Park was opened in Argyll, Scotland. Following the Forestry Act 1967, the Forestry Commission was empowered to provide tourism and recreational facilities on its property and nowadays the Commission's forests attract over 50 million day visits each year. The Commission also manages thirty camping and caravan sites and four holiday cabin developments.

The aim of current forestry policy within the UK is to integrate the needs of tourism, conservation and landscape improvement with the more traditional purpose of timber production. That is, forests are now viewed as a multi-purpose resource and evidence of this is to be found in recent developments. In particular, the purpose of the new National Forest and, on a smaller scale, twelve Community Forests in England (Figure 2.1) is to reclaim derelict industrial and agricultural land and, through the development of woods, meadows and small housing developments, to create new, green areas that will serve a variety of purposes, including conservation, education and recreation.

Water

Water resources, whether natural (rivers, lakes or coastal waters) or man-made (reservoirs and canals) are an integral feature of many rural areas and, like the countryside as a whole, support a variety of uses. In addition to satisfying domestic, industrial and agricultural demands, they play an essential role in flood control and land drainage, they are a source of food, they frequently represent an important element of a country's transport network, and they are of fundamental importance to nature and wildlife conservation.

Water is also, of course, an important resource for tourism and leisure (McCormack 1994). In many countries, for example, inland waterways are used for a variety of activities, such as sailing, canoeing, rowing or cruising holidays. White-water rafting is becoming increasingly popular in countries as diverse as the United States, Nepal and Zimbabwe, whilst an enormous variety of other activities, including fishing, water-skiing and diving, take place on both inland and coastal waters. Furthermore, it is not only the use of the water itself that attracts visitors; riverbanks, beaches, cliffs and lakesides support a number of activities, such as walking, painting, photography or bird-watching, all of which to a lesser or greater extent depend on the water environment.

Given this enormous range of demands placed upon water resources, it is not surprising that conflicts frequently occur between different demands and activities. For example, motorised water sports conflict with 'quieter' activities, such as fishing, whilst, in countries where water is in short supply, decisions have to be made about the most appropriate use of a scarce resource. However, in one sense water resources also represent a demand on the wider countryside because the building of canals or the creation of reservoirs effectively 'uses up' the countryside. Most new schemes to build dams to create reservoirs are met with strong national and, frequently, international opposition from the conservation lobby, although this is not a new phenomenon. In

Figure 2.1 The National Forest and Community Forests in England

1919, for example, the US National Park Service successfully fought off a total of four separate water development projects in just one national park, Yellowstone (Albright and Cahn 1985), whilst, during the 1870s, an eventually successful bid by the then Manchester Water Corporation to transform Thirlmere in the English Lake District into a large reservoir was met with fierce opposition (Berry and Beard 1980). Not only was the level of the lake raised by fifty feet, submerging two small villages and several farms, but also virtually no access has been permitted to either the lake or the surrounding forest since 1890 (Rollinson 1967). Thus, water is both an important resource satisfying a variety of demands and uses whilst also representing a demand on the wider countryside. (See Tanner 1993 for a detailed assessment of water resources and their leisure use in the UK.)

Housing

A major feature of the nineteenth century was the rapid urbanisation of many Western societies. For example, in 1800, 80 per cent of the population of the UK lived in rural areas; by 1900, following widespread migration into towns and cities, just 20 per cent of the population remained in the countryside. In recent years the trend has reversed as, in a process referred to as counter-urbanisation, increasing numbers of people have been moving out of urban areas to live in the countryside. Of course, the extent to which counter-urbanisation occurs varies according to national or regional characteristics; some countries, such as those in the former eastern bloc, are still experiencing migration into urban areas, whilst others, particularly in northern Europe, have witnessed a significant growth in rural-based housing developments since the 1970s. However, the ever-increasing need for land for housing developments, either on the urban–rural fringe or within the countryside, represents a significant demand on the countryside.

Importantly, it is not only spatially that housing uses up the countryside. As Hoggart *et al.* (1995: 249) point out, counter-urbanisation in Europe has also transformed the social and cultural characteristics of rural areas whilst, perhaps inevitably, the visual and amenity quality of the countryside is affected. Herein lies a paradox, for it is often the perceived quality and character of life in the rural environment that motivates people to move out from urban areas into the countryside, yet in doing so they contribute to the dilution or elimination of those elements of rurality which they seek (Aslet 1991).

Conservation and environmental protection

Although its roots lie in the nineteenth century, it is only during the latter half of the twentieth century that what may be described as the environmental movement has achieved international prominence and recognition. Since the 1960s the environmental lobby has experienced a widespread increase in support and membership (Lowe and Goyder 1983), green parties have emerged on the political scene and a number of international commissions and conferences, such as the World Commission on Environment and Development (WCED 1987) and the 1992 Rio Earth Summit, have positioned the environment high on the international political agenda.

The attention of this environmental movement has been focused both on global issues, such as the destruction of the ozone layer and the so-called 'greenhouse effect', and on more specific forms of resource exploitation or economic activity. Not the least, the emergence and growth of mass tourism has been mirrored by increasing concern about its impacts on the physical and socio-cultural environment in destination areas (Mathieson and Wall 1982; Croall 1995) whilst, generally, the relationship between tourism and its environment is a matter of intense debate (Hunter and Green 1995). It is also, arguably, one of the most important challenges facing the future development of tourism and the concept of sustainable tourism development is introduced in the final section of this chapter.

However, within the context of the rural environment in particular, the issue of conservation and protection considerably pre-dates the current global prominence of the environmental movement. Since the Industrial Revolution which, particularly in the northern European countries, 'polarized urban and rural differences' (Hoggart *et al.* 1995:229), conservation has increasingly represented a demand on the countryside in the sense that, although it does not diminish the 'supply' of countryside, it nevertheless restricts other uses (Sharpley 1996). Initially, conservation efforts were motivated simply by the desire to protect rural areas from creeping urbanisation and industrialisation (i.e. resource exploitation) but, as the potential of the countryside as a resource for tourism and leisure became recognised, conservation in the countryside increasingly adopted a dual role. For example, since the designation of the world's first national park at Yellowstone in 1872, most national parks have served both conservation and recreation purposes. A variety of other forms of land designation have also been adopted depending on the level or type of human activity permitted and, since 1970, the area of protected land in many countries has grown significantly (Table 2.2). Currently about 4 per cent of the world's

Table 2.2 Protected areas

	(1000 sq km)				% land area
	1970	1980	1985	1989	1989
Canada	148.2	214.6	229.5	718.6	7.8
USA	234.5	473.9	649.5	790.4	8.6
Japan	19.7	21.3	22.0	24.0	6.4
Australia	108.6	250.7	354.1	364.8	4.8
New Zealand	25.5	26.2	27.9	28.3	10.6
Austria	2.6	2.6	3.0	15.9	19.3
Belgium	0.0	0.0	0.1	0.8	2.6
Denmark	0.1	0.1	1.3	2.8	6.7
Finland	4.8	4.8	8.0	8.1	2.6
France	4.7	12.8	16.5	45.0	8.2
W. Germany	1.3	2.9	5.3	27.6	11.3
Ireland	0.1	0.1	0.2	0.2	0.4
Italy	3.0	4.1	5.2	12.7	4.3
Netherlands	0.9	1.1	1.6	1.5	4.4
Norway	2.1	37.9	47.2	47.6	15.5
Portugal	0.7	2.5	3.8	6.2	6.7
Spain	9.2	16.8	17.0	25.6	5.1
Sweden	5.0	10.6	15.9	17.1	4.2
Switzerland	0.2	0.2	1.2	1.2	3.0
Turkey	0.5	2.3	2.9	2.5	0.3
UK	13.0	13.2	15.5	25.7	10.6
World	**1597.1**	**3566.2**	**4237.7**	**5290.8**	**4.0**

Source: OECD 1991

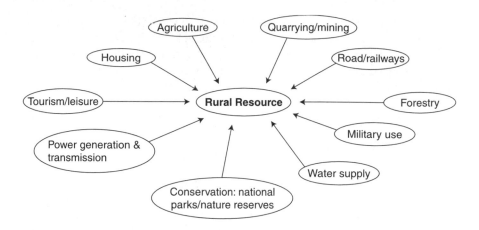

Figure 2.2 Demands on the rural resource

land area is protected under International Union for the Conservation of Nature (IUCN) recognised designations, a figure which rises to 7.1 per cent if only OECD countries are included (OECD 1991).

More recently, the concept of protecting the countryside has broadened into the conservation of 'rurality'. That is, rural conservation is seen to include the protection of rural society and culture and, significantly, tourism is being increasingly promoted as a means of achieving this through both its potential for employment and income creation and its contribution to wildlife and landscape conservation.

There are, of course, a variety of other demands or uses which make a claim on the countryside, demonstrating the multi-purpose nature of the resource. For example, mineral extraction, power generation and transmission, military training and the provision of transport facilities, such as road building, are all legitimate demands which share the countryside with those outlined above (Figure 2.2). Importantly, a number of these uses are becoming less mutually exclusive and tourism, in particular, is playing an increasingly important role in sharing and sustaining the use of the countryside. However, farming remains the primary use of the countryside and it is important, therefore, to consider the changing relationship between tourism and agricultural policy.

TOURISM, AGRICULTURE AND RURAL DEVELOPMENT POLICY

The development and promotion of rural tourism is frequently justified on the basis of its potential contribution to the social and economic regeneration of rural areas. For example, throughout rural Europe tourism is now considered to be an important new source of income and employment at the same time as fulfilling the broader role of breaking down social isolation and encouraging the repopulation of rural communities (Cavaco 1995). In other words, tourism is often seen as the solution to many of the problems facing farmers around the world.

This arguably excessive faith in the developmental role of rural tourism has arisen, it has been suggested, as a result of misconceptions about its focus and applicability (OECD 1994). In particular, as pointed out in Chapter 1, rural tourism encompasses a broad range of activities yet it is often seen to be synonymous with farm tourism. In some countries, especially southern Germany, there is a long tradition of rural tourism based largely on accommodation on farms (Opperman 1996) but the particular set of conditions, such as accessibility, scenery and availability of suitable accommodation, that have made German farm tourism a success do not necessarily exist in other agricultural areas. For example, there is relatively little evidence of farm tourism in Scandinavia or North America. Furthermore, many forms of rural tourism occur in non-agricultural or wilderness areas whilst in some countries, such as the UK, the great majority of rural tourists are on day visits, limiting the potential economic benefits.

Nevertheless, particularly within the European context, there is an identifiable relationship between the promotion of rural tourism, agricultural policies and broader, regional development policies, demonstrating an increasing recognition of the countryside as a resource for tourism. This has resulted, to a great extent, from recent changes to the Common Agricultural Policy (CAP) which have presented rural communities throughout the European Union (EU) with a variety of challenges and opportunities. It is important, therefore, to consider briefly the objectives of the CAP and its links with the development of rural tourism.

The Common Agricultural Policy and rural tourism

The CAP is probably one of the most controversial of all EU policies. Despite agriculture accounting for just 2.4 per cent of GDP and 6.5 per cent of employment in the EU, the CAP's price support mechanism accounts for almost half of the entire EU annual budget (Nugent 1994) and it is frequently criticised for subsidising already wealthy farmers, for creating farm surpluses in the form of 'butter mountains' and 'wine lakes', and for resulting in high prices for consumers. It has also kept European prices for agricultural products high relative to world prices and there has, therefore, been strong pressure on the EU from other countries, particularly the United States, to reduce the level of subsidies. Nevertheless, many would argue that some form of agricultural policy in Europe is both desirable and necessary and, despite widespread criticism, the CAP has achieved some of its objectives.

In its original form, the CAP was intended to increase agricultural production, to maintain a fair standard of living for farmers, to stabilise markets and to ensure a constant supply of farm products at a reasonable price to the consumer. The main way of achieving these objectives has been through a pricing mechanism which, essentially, guarantees the price paid to European farmers for many products. A target price is set at which, it is hoped, farmers are able to sell their produce on the world market. If the world price falls below this, then the EU buys up surplus produce to maintain European prices to farmers. The cost of this support is met by the European Agricultural Guidance and Guarantee Fund (EAGGF), which falls into two parts; the guarantee section finances price support schemes and the smaller guidance fund is directed towards structural schemes, such as support for the introduction of more efficient farming techniques.

As a result of this support, leading to high guaranteed prices and more efficient, intensive farming methods, many products have been produced in amounts surplus to EU requirements; for example, in the early 1990s, cereals, vegetables, dairy products and poultry were all being produced well in excess of total EU requirements. Thus, although farmers' incomes have remained comparable to other sectors and self-sufficiency in food production has been achieved, large surpluses have had to be disposed of at a huge cost. At the same time, the contribution of agriculture to both rural employment and GDP in EU states has steadily declined.

In order to reduce the large and costly production surpluses a number of reforms to the CAP were introduced in 1992. Since then, support prices have been reduced, set-aside schemes, where farmers are paid to take a proportion of arable land out of production, have been set up and farmers have been given financial incentives for early retirement or to adopt more environmentally friendly farming methods. These reforms have gone some way to reducing the problem of surplus production, but the CAP still remains a contentious issue both within the EU and amongst other countries which consider the EU agricultural sector to be overprotected and over subsidised (see Nugent 1994 for a detailed assessment of the CAP).

Throughout its existence, the CAP has influenced the development of rural tourism. Initially, the emphasis on efficient production methods led to falling employment within the agricultural sector which not only encouraged migration into urban areas but also, indirectly, led to a reduction in rural services. Since 1992, large amounts of rural land have also become available for other uses (see Baldock and Beaufoy 1993) and, with the reduction in support prices, farmers have been obliged to look for alternative land uses and sources of income. As a result, tourism has been widely promoted throughout Europe (Pompl and Lavery 1993; Williams and Shaw 1991) and has become increasingly relied upon as a means of reversing economic and social decline in rural areas (Hannigan 1994a). This has occurred most frequently in marginal areas which have been least able to accommodate the changes in the CAP and, in some countries, the promotion of rural tourism has been directly supported at the national level. For example, in the UK the Countryside Stewardship scheme, introduced in 1991, is designed to promote conservation and recreation on surplus rural lands (Countryside Commission 1991a), whilst organisations such as the Rural Development Commission, the Ministry of Agriculture, Fisheries and Food, the Forestry Commission and the English Tourist Board (ETB 1988) actively promote and support the development of rural tourism (Sharpley 1996). However, it is important to note that tourism should not be simply regarded as 'the systematic consequences of the difficulties encountered by agricultural policies' (Greffe 1994) as regional and structural development plans throughout the EU have also influenced the development of rural tourism.

Structural funds and rural tourism in the EU

The structural development of rural areas in the EU is supported in part by the guidance section of the EAGGF, but the major sources of finance for such development are the European Regional Development Fund (ERDF) and the European Social Fund (ESF). The overall purpose of these funds is to promote economic and social development in those regions which are considered to be falling behind other regions. The specific objectives are:

1. The development of structurally backward regions.
2. The conversion of regions in industrial decline.
3. The combating of long-term employment.
4. The increase of employment opportunities for young people.
5. (a) the adjustment of agricultural structures to accompany the reform of the CAP;
   (b) the promotion of the development of rural areas.

Regions falling under the category of Objective 1 are those regions where *per capita* GDP falls under 75 per cent of the EU average and together comprise over 40 per cent of the total land area, but around 22 per cent of the population, of the EU. Objective 5(b) regions are much smaller, covering about 5 per cent of the total population, but together they represent a significant source of funding for the development of rural areas. Objective 5(b) funding is of particular relevance to rural tourism development because, although it finances a wide variety of rural developments, tourism projects are frequent recipients of funding. Furthermore, between 1989 and 1993, 5.5 per cent of the Community Structural Funds allocated to Objective 1 regions were invested directly in tourism development projects (Hannigan 1994a). The development of tourism in the Republic of Ireland, described in Case study 2, is one example of where tourism has been supported by European funding in order to revitalise the economy and to strengthen the country's economic position within Europe. It also demonstrates that care must be taken not to over-estimate the potential economic benefits resulting from the development of tourism.

Case study 2: Tourism development in the Republic of Ireland

The Republic of Ireland is the second smallest and one of the poorest countries in the EU (Hannigan 1994b). Classified as an Objective 1 region, per capita GDP remains at less than 70 per cent of the EU average (see Page 1994), *per capita* income is also below the European average and, in the early 1990s, the unemployment rate reached almost 20 per cent amongst its population of 3.5 million (Deegan and Dineen 1993). These economic problems have resulted, in part, from the country's continuing dependence on agriculture, but a manufacturing sector with a significant proportion of foreign-owned companies where 'repatriation of profits is the norm' (Hurley *et al*. 1994) and a rapidly increasing population have exacerbated the problem. Nevertheless, during the late 1980s and the early 1990s, the Irish Republic's tourism industry experienced rapid expansion, largely as a result of the high priority given to the industry by the government and the significant financial support from European structural funds. Indeed, since the mid-1980s the Irish government has adopted a 'relatively interventionist' stance towards tourism (EIU 1991), viewing it as an effective vehicle for development in the more lagging parts of the country.

The Irish tourism industry has not always enjoyed rapid growth. The Republic was a popular destination during the 1960s, sharing the boom in international tourism experienced by many other destinations, but the continuing expansion in tourism elsewhere was not mirrored in Ireland during the 1970s and 1980s. In fact, earnings in real terms from tourism in the early 1980s were below those in the late 1960s and, between 1969 and 1972, visitor numbers fell by a quarter (Gillmor 1994). In comparison, earnings from tourism in the UK rose by almost 300 per cent in the twenty years up to 1985. The initial fall in tourism resulted almost entirely from the outbreak of violence in Northern Ireland in 1969 but the continuing stagnation in tourism to Ireland can be attributed to a number of other factors, including high inflation, which made the country relatively expensive to visit, and a lack of investment in tourism facilities.

However, in 1987, following the publication of a number of reports into tourism in Ireland, the government seized upon tourism for its economic and employment development potential. The 'Programme for National Recovery' set the objective of doubling the number of overseas visitors to Ireland within the next five years in order to create an extra 25,000 jobs and to attract an additional IR£500 million in tourist spending. Initially, this was to be achieved by improving air access to the country, aggressive marketing and investment incentives, such as tax breaks, through extending the Business Expansion Scheme. By 1991, Bord Fáilte, (the Irish Tourist Board) had approved 275 tourism development projects (EIU 1991) and had also extensively promoted agritourism in order to encourage rural economic development. In 1989, however, the EC approved Ireland's 'Operational Plan for Tourism 1989–93' in line with the aims of the Single European Act (see Hurley *et al*. 1994) and further support for tourism development was provided directly from European Structural Funds, in particular from the European Regional Development Fund which provided almost half of the IR£218 million grant-aid to tourism projects between 1989 and 1993 (Hannigan 1994b).

There is no doubt that the strategy was successful in reversing the

Table 2.3 Tourist arrivals and receipts in Ireland 1987–91

Year	Arrivals ('000s)	Receipts (IR£m)
1987	2664	731
1988	3007	841
1989	3484	991
1990	3666	1139
1991	3535	1213

Source: Hurley *et al.* (1994)

trend of low growth in tourist arrivals and receipts. From 1987, tourist arrivals in Ireland increased at about 10 per cent per annum and revenue from tourism increased accordingly (Table 2.3)

Furthermore, in terms of employment creation, the strategy also appears to have been successful. The original targets of the Programme for National Recovery were almost met during the five years to 1993, with an estimated 15,327 direct and 8939 indirect full time-equivalent jobs being created (Hurley *et al.* 1994). Based on this, a further commitment to tourism development and to further growth in tourist arrivals and receipts was made in the second Operational Plan for Tourism 1994–99, which forecast the creation of a further 35,000 jobs by 1999. Recent figures suggest that the growth in arrivals and foreign exchange earnings has continued as forecast (Table 2.4).

However, the apparent success of the tourism development strategy and the potential for future growth must be approached with some caution, for a number of reasons:

● Despite the continued growth in overall arrivals, only 42 per cent of overseas visitors in 1995 had a holiday as the main purpose of their visit, whilst 21 per cent were travelling on business and 23 per cent were visiting friends or relatives.
● It has been suggested that much of the growth in tourism to Ireland has resulted as much from favourable economic conditions in Europe in the late 1980s and mid-1990s, the widespread growth in second/third holidays and short breaks and the greater interest in rural/green holidays as from the actual policies of Bord Fáilte.
● The objective of increasing the spending per visitor in order to attain revenue targets is also unlikely to be met as average expenditure per visitor has not increased since 1987 (Hannigan 1994b).
● Many of the jobs created, particularly in the poorer, western regions, have been lower-grade and seasonal or part-time; conversely, the richer, eastern seaboard attracted a higher proportion of full-time jobs.

Table 2.4 Tourist arrivals and receipts in Ireland 1993–95

Year	Arrivals ('000s)	Receipts (IR£m)
1993	3888	1367
1994	4309	1498
1995	4821	1677

Source: Bord Fáilte (1996)

Table 2.5 Overseas* tourist numbers and revenue in Ireland by region, 1995

Region	Number ('000s)	Revenue (IR£m)
Dublin	2264	433.9
Midlands-east	792	138.2
South-east	953	135.6
South-west	1287	243.1
Mid-west	876	134.9
West	1052	169.3
North-west	752	112.0

* Includes arrivals from Northern Ireland
Source: Bord Fáilte

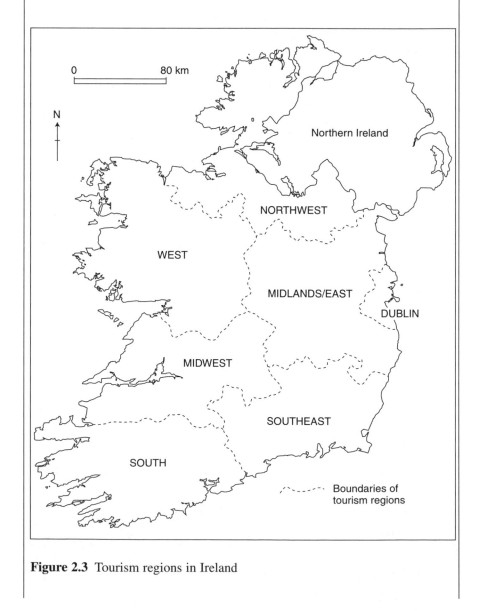

Figure 2.3 Tourism regions in Ireland

● The distribution of tourism in the Republic of Ireland is traditionally uneven, with Dublin and the south-west region (Table 2.5 and Figure 2.3) attracting the highest proportion of visitors. Thus, those areas which already benefited from tourism experienced high growth rates between 1987 and 1991 whilst other regions remained less popular. This pattern has continued, with Dublin and the south-west regions attracting almost 50 per cent of tourism receipts in 1995.

Together, these points imply that the economic and employment creation objectives of developing tourism in the Republic of Ireland, particularly in the poorer, rural areas, have not been achieved. Although it has been a valuable component in the social and economic development of some rural areas, surveys have shown that the benefits have not been uniform, with the midlands and north-west regions experiencing the least benefit. Conversely, Dublin, although the smallest tourism region by area, consistently earns the greatest share of total revenue (over 31 per cent in 1995) from tourism, followed by the western part of the country which, as a result of its traditional culture and attractive scenery, has long been of greatest appeal to tourists. Moreover, the pattern of bedspace availability reflects the regional spread of tourism, which itself reflects the distribution of attractions, different levels of investment and development and the location of tourist gateways around the Republic. It is also suggested (Gillmor 1994: 26) that this regional spread of tourism would be even more marked if it were not for the high level of VFR (Visiting Friends and Relatives) tourism which is less influenced by the distribution of traditional tourism attractions and resources and, overall, these factors call into question the value of grant-aid for tourism development and highlight the potential for over-dependence on tourism in regional development.

Note: See Kockel (1994) for a complete analysis of tourism development in Ireland

However, one EU rural development scheme that is of particular interest in the context of tourism is the LEADER programme (see Nitsch and van Straaten 1995). First established in 1990 and now continuing as LEADER II, the programme (Liaisons Entre Actions pour la Développement des Économies Rurales) is intended to promote an integrated approach to rural development, with particular emphasis on local support and involvement. Local Action Groups are formed and, once a business development plan has been approved, the groups receive and disburse funding from EU structural funds, as well as national and private sector funding. Of the 217 LEADER areas in the EU as a whole, tourism is the dominant business plan in 71 (Calatrava and Avilés 1993) and in Spain, tourism is the main activity in 36 out of 52 local groups (Barke and Newton 1994; 1995). Case study 3 describes a LEADER funded project in South Pembrokeshire, Wales.

Case study 3: Tourism and the SPARC Project

In 1987, the Taf and Cleddau Rural Initiative (TCRI) was established as a pilot project to improve the social and economic well-being of 18 rural communities based around the market towns of Narbeth and Whitland in south Pembrokeshire, Wales (Figure 2.4). In 1992, following a successful bid for LEADER funding, the TCRI model was extended to the whole of rural south Pembrokeshire, covering some 35 rural towns and villages, and was re-named the South Pembrokeshire Partnership for Action with Rural Communities (SPARC).

The area covered by SPARC is a rural area in the south-west of Wales and, being predominantly agricultural with a low level of socio-economic development, below average GDP and unemployment of almost 17 per cent, it met EC criteria for special funding. The project's overall aim was to work towards rural development based upon local community involvement and partnerships with local government and other agencies, and it was supported by funding from a variety of sources other than the LEADER programme, including the Wales Tourist Board.

A total of 35 villages created Community Associations which, through a process of local consultation, produced local action plans for development. Within these plans, individual projects were devised which were then assessed by SPARC according to a set of selection criteria, including:

- contribution to the area's tourism strategy;
- contribution to growth in existing or new economic sectors;

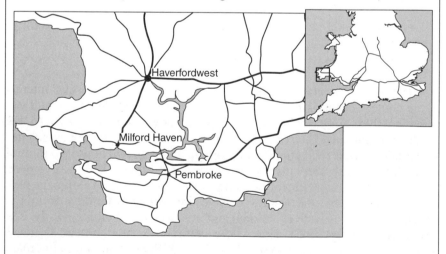

Figure 2.4 The SPARC project area

- beneficial economic impact to local communities;
- benefit to local community in respect of leisure, social and recreational activities.

Such was the immediate success of the project that over 1000 people regularly worked with SPARC for the benefit of their communities and over 100 different projects were approved. Although projects related to a variety of themes, including agriculture and forestry, craft enterprises and vocational training, were proposed, many were related to the development of rural tourism. Indeed, tourism was considered to be an important but relatively untapped mechanism for diversification of the local economy and the SPARC Rural Tourism Strategy represented the major recipient of project funding. Many projects were inter-linking, such as the 80 kilometre Landsker Borderlands Trail, a themed circular walk linking all the communities, but individual communities also researched and produced information leaflets or panels based on the local heritage. A variety of other tourism related projects were undertaken, including the development of a visitor centre and the establishment of a walking festival, and the overall success of the tourism strategy was recognised when the Landsker Borderlands, as the SPARC project area was themed, won the prestigious Tourism for Tomorrow award in 1994.

There is little doubt that, in many cases, tourism can represent a fruitful new 'cash crop' for rural areas within the LEADER programme. For example, the proportion of employment in the service sector in the Alpujarras region near Granada in southern Spain grew from 25 per cent to 66 per cent between 1982 and 1992. This was mirrored by a fall in the contribution of farming to employment from 70 per cent to 38 per cent, whilst the supply of accommodation more than doubled and income from tourism and related activities increased twelve-fold during the same period (Calatrava and Avilés 1993). However, it has also been suggested that, rather than helping farms to survive, the development of tourism has actually accelerated the decline in farming in the region, indicating that, despite the attraction of tourism as a rural development option, it may lead to problems in the longer term (Barke and Newton 1994).

Efforts to utilise the countryside as a resource for tourism are also evident in other parts of the world, although not to the same extent as in Europe. Studies in the United States, for example, have found that 30 states have tourism programmes specifically for rural areas, a further 14 states included rural tourism within their overall tourism development plans and just 6 states had no rural tourism strategy (Luloff *et al.* 1994). Most of the programmes, however, were based upon marketing and promotion schemes rather than product development and were unconnected with broader economic and social development objectives. Thus, although rural areas in the United States have suffered the same problems as those in other countries, 'rural tourism as an economic development strategy is more rhetoric than action' (Luloff *et al.* 1994). Only five states have designed tourism programmes with the specific purpose of promoting rural economic development, indicating that a more comprehensive and integrated approach, such as the European LEADER programme, is required if tourism is to achieve its potential as a means of regenerating rural areas. Nevertheless, the development of rural tourism is generally justified on the basis of its contribution to social and economic development and it is necessary, therefore, to outline both the potential benefits and costs of exploiting the countryside as a resource for tourism.

RURAL TOURISM DEVELOPMENT: THE BENEFITS

The over-riding purpose of all tourism development, whether international or domestic, is the potential for economic and social development in destination areas. Many, if not most, countries around the world have embraced tourism to a greater or lesser extent and the importance of tourism in the global economy is frequently expressed in terms of its contribution to income and employment. Thus, it has been estimated that, as the world's largest industry, tourism is worth some $3.4 trillion and accounts for 10.1 per cent of world GDP and 10.6 per cent of world employment (WTTC 1994). Rural tourism is, of course, a relatively small sector of this total world market for tourism, yet it still makes a significant contribution to rural economies. For example, it has been suggested that rural tourism in England generates about £9 billion annually (Countryside Commission 1995b) and, in some parts of the country, is the dominant source of employment.

However, measuring the benefits of tourism simply in terms of gross output and employment figures hides a number of broader economic, social and environmental benefits that can result from the development of tourism in rural areas. These are summarised below (see also Broom 1992; Gannon 1994; OECD 1994).

Economic benefits

Rural tourism represents an important additional or new source of income to rural communities. As a result:

- new jobs may be created in tourism related businesses, such as accommodation, catering, retailing, transport and entertainment;
- existing employment opportunities in services, such as transport, hospitality or medical care, and in more traditional rural industries and crafts are safeguarded;
- the local economy becomes diversified, providing a broader and more stable economic base for the local community;
- opportunities for pluriactivity may emerge, thereby guarding against recession and protecting income levels;

- existing businesses and services are supported;
- new businesses may be attracted to the area, further diversifying and strengthening the local economy whilst reducing the need for state subsidy of farming.

Social benefits

The development of rural tourism contributes to a variety of social benefits to rural communities, including:

- the maintenance and support of local services, such as public transport and health care;
- new facilities and attractions, such as cultural or entertainment facilities or sports centres;
- increased social contact in more isolated communities and opportunities for cultural exchange;
- greater awareness and the revitalisation of local customs, crafts and cultural identities;
- the re-population of rural areas, reversing the trend towards declining and older rural communities;
- the development of the role of women in more traditional or isolated rural communities (Shaw and Williams 1994: 238).

Environmental benefits

For many tourists, the prime motivation for visiting the countryside is the rural environment. The success of rural tourism development depends upon an attractive environment and, therefore, tourism:

- provides both the financial resources and the stimulus for the conservation, protection and improvement of the natural rural environment;
- supports the preservation and improvement of the historic built environment, including country houses, gardens and parklands. (Tourism also leads to the re-development of old, redundant buildings in the countryside; for example, old warehouses or mills can be converted into craft centres or old barns can be converted into accommodation units);
- leads to environmental improvements in rural towns and villages, such as litter disposal, traffic regulation and general improvements to buildings.

RURAL TOURISM DEVELOPMENT: THE COSTS

The countryside is a resource that is exploited for a variety of purposes and, inevitably, all these uses have some negative impact on the resource. Thus, 'the countryside's tourism potential cannot be tapped without costs, effects on the environment and risks of depletion' (Thibal 1988: 13). Indeed, all forms of tourism, including rural tourism, negatively impact to some extent upon the physical and socio-cultural environment in destination areas and, since the 1970s, increasing attention has been paid to ways of developing more sustainable forms of tourism. This issue is considered in more detail in Chapter 6 but, just as there are potential benefits resulting from the development of rural tourism, so too are there potential costs or negative impacts. Whilst the level of these impacts varies according to a number of factors, including the size and importance of the local tourism industry, the volume of tourists and their activities, the robustness of the local environment and the strength of local cultures and traditions, some or all of the following costs may be associated with the development of tourism in the countryside.

Economic costs

Whilst tourism undoubtedly contributes to income and employment opportunities, these benefits must be balanced against potential economic costs. In particular, rural tourism:

- increases the demand for, and cost of, public services, such as refuse collection, medical services and the police;
- incurs developmental costs, including attractions, facilities and general infrastructural improvements;
- may create jobs which are part-time or seasonal. (Furthermore, local people may neither wish, nor possess the relevant skills, to respond to the employment opportunities offered by tourism with the result that many tourism-related businesses are run by 'outsiders');
- frequently leads to increases in the price of land, property, goods and services. (In particular, holiday-home ownership in rural areas often means that local people are no longer able to afford the cost of housing);
- may result in local communities becoming over-dependent on a single industry, the success of which is beyond the control of the local community. (For example, prolonged bad weather or competition from other areas may reduce the number of visitors, undermining the longer-term economic viability of tourism).

Social costs

The influx of large numbers of tourists can have both short- and longer-term impacts on the social and cultural stability of rural communities. It has long been accepted that tourism can act as a catalyst in the process of acculturation (Nuñez 1989; Sharpley 1994: 214) with traditional, remote and small-scale rural communities being particularly susceptible to outside influence. However, tourism development may result in more specific negative effects on local societies and culture, including:

- increases in crime and other antisocial behaviour;
- congestion and crowding which impinges on the day to day life and privacy of local residents;

- a reduction in local services, such as the replacement of traditional shops with restaurants or souvenir shops;
- the introduction of new ideas, styles and behavioural modes which challenge traditional culture and values;
- pressures on housing availability and conflict between locals and incoming temporary or permanent residents.

Environmental costs

The rural environment is particularly fragile and susceptible to the development of tourism. Generally, the presence of large numbers of visitors and the provision of attractions and facilities to satisfy their needs may, if not properly controlled or managed, diminish or even destroy the very characteristics that attract tourists to rural areas in the first place. In particular, tourism:

- causes damage to both the natural and man-made environment. (Activities such as skiing, hiking, rock-climbing and riding all have an impact on the physical environment, whilst country houses, gardens and parks may suffer from intensive visitor use);
- increases the level of pollution in rural areas. (This may be physical pollution, such as litter and rubbish, air pollution from excessive amounts of traffic, noise pollution, or visual pollution resulting from, for example, traffic jams on country roads or developments which are inappropriate or intrude upon the rural setting).

CONCLUSION

The countryside is a resource which supports a variety of demands and uses, including tourism. Some of these uses, such as farming and forestry, are an integral element of the physical and social characteristics of the countryside whereas other demands, such as housing or road building, effectively use up or diminish the overall supply of countryside. Importantly, however, these demands are not mutually exclusive; not only is the countryside a finite resource, implying that it must be shared amongst all the various demands placed upon it, but also each demand or use directly influences the viability of other uses. The more that one use dominates the countryside, the less able are other uses to exploit the resource.

In short, a relationship exists between all the demands on the countryside and, as greater and more diverse demands are placed on the countryside, the nature of that relationship is also changing. In particular, as the contribution of agriculture to employment and income generation continues to decline, tourism is being increasingly viewed as a viable and justifiable economic activity in rural areas. No longer simply tolerated by rural communities, tourism is now actively promoted as the new 'cash crop', the panacea to the economic problems facing rural areas. At the same time, tourism is also becoming increasingly integrated with other demands and activities, such as forestry, water supply and conservation, demonstrating not only an inter-relationship but also an inter-dependence between the different uses of the rural resource.

The success of rural tourism, however, is reliant upon the maintenance of a healthy and attractive rural environment. Implicitly, therefore, there is a need to effectively manage and balance all the various demands on the countryside whilst also ensuring that tourism itself is not permitted to diminish the qualities and attractions of the resource upon which it depends. Thus, it is also important to understand the characteristics of the demand for rural tourism and the ways in which these demands can be satisfied. These issues are considered in the following chapters.

QUESTIONS

1. How have the demands and pressures on the rural resource base changed and increased over time?
2. Why, in many rural areas, has tourism come to be seen as the new 'cash crop'?
3. How effective do you consider tourism to be as a vehicle for the socio-economic development of the countryside?
4. What are the benefits and costs of rural tourism development?

FURTHER READING

Bouquet, M. and Winter, M. (1987) *Who From their Labours Rest? Conflict and Practice in Rural Tourism*, Aldershot: Avebury.

Bramwell, B. and Lane, B. (1994) *Rural Tourism and Sustainable Rural Development,* Bristol: Channel View Publications.

Cavaco, C. (1995) Rural Tourism: The Creation of New Tourist Spaces, in A. Montanari, and A. Williams (eds), *European Tourism: Regions, Spaces and Restructuring*, Chichester: John Wiley & Sons.

Glyptis, S. (1991) *Countryside Recreation*, Harlow: Longman.

Mathieson, A. and Wall, G. (1982) *Tourism: Economic, Physical and Social Impacts*, Harlow: Longman.

OECD (1993) *What Future for Our Countryside? A Rural Development Policy*, Paris: Organisation for Economic Co-operation and Development.

The demand for rural tourism | 3

INTRODUCTION

The measurement and understanding of the demand for tourism is of fundamental importance to the overall tourism planning and management process. Without accurate information and figures relating to the historical, current and forecast demand for tourism, governments, tourism agencies and individual tourism operators would be unable, for example, to formulate policies, plan marketing and promotional campaigns or make effective investment decisions. Therefore, it is not surprising that, in most tourist destination areas, much emphasis is placed on the collection and analysis of tourism data on a national, regional and, sometimes, local basis.

Generally, the data collected measure the actual demand for tourism and are expressed in terms of figures relating to a variety of criteria. Thus, many countries publish annual figures detailing the number and nationality of international arrivals, the purpose of their visit, where and how long they stay and how much they spend and, each year, these figures are collated and published by the World Tourism Organisation (WTO). In this way, the annual demand for international tourism as a whole is measured by the total number of visitor arrivals and total spending which, according to the WTO, amounted in 1994 to over 531 million arrivals who generated tourism revenue totalling some $321 billion (WTO 1995).

There are a number of advantages to be gained from this statistical measurement of the demand for tourism. For example, it provides an overall picture of the development, growth and value of tourism as an international industry and it allows individual countries to compare their performance as a tourist destination with that of other countries. Similarly, within countries or destinations it indicates the value of tourism as a sector of the national economy and the relative performance of different sectors of the tourism industry.

However, there are also a number of problems associated with the quantitative measurement of tourism. For example, it is widely accepted that, as a result of different survey methods and measurement criteria adopted in different countries, the meaningful analysis and interpretation of tourism statistics is fraught with difficulties. Differences in sample sizes, sample selection methods and the regularity of surveys all create difficulties whilst, at a more fundamental level, comparable data depend upon internationally accepted definitions of tourism and tourist activities. Thus, when considering the volume of international tourism, what is impressive is not the size of the figure 'but the fact that anybody should know its value or be able to work it out' (Cooper *et al.* 1993: 57).

The measurement of the demand for rural tourism in particular is beset with similar problems. As discussed in Chapter 1, rural tourism comprises a vast range of activities and pursuits, some of which, such as visits to managed attractions or destinations, are relatively easy to quantify. However, participation in many other activities is spontaneous and informal and, therefore, much more difficult to measure. At the same time, differing definitions of countryside and conflicting views amongst survey respondents as to what actually constitutes rural tourism may further complicate attempts to accurately assess the level of demand for tourism in the countryside. Thus, in the absence of continuous and large scale surveys based upon internationally agreed definitions and criteria, statistics which express the demand for rural tourism are likely to be, at best, reasonable estimates (Sharpley 1996: 60).

Perhaps of more importance, statistical measurements of the volume and value of rural tourism, irrespective of their accuracy, provide a useful basis for comparing the popularity of different rural destinations or the contribution of tourism to the local economy, but they are of less worth within the context of planning and managing rural tourism. In other words, if the market for rural tourism is to be fully exploited and the greatest advantage to be gained from its development, it is important to understand the 'who, where, when and why' of rural tourism. As Curry (1994: 83) argues, 'a more general understanding of people's participation patterns provides a crucial input to policy formulation for countryside recreation and access' and a consideration of demand factors such as motivation, perceptions and frequency of participation is, therefore, essential to the planning process.

The purpose of this chapter is to outline briefly the historical development and to examine the defining characteristics of the demand for rural tourism. It identifies a number of broader factors that may influence this demand and suggests that effective planning and management is dependent on the recognition and understanding of these factors. Initially, however, it is important to clarify the criteria by which rural tourism may be measured, particularly in terms of the length of a visit.

RURAL TOURISM: MEASUREMENT CRITERIA

It is evident that it is difficult to accurately define what is meant by rural tourism, although it may generally be described as a form of tourism that occurs in rural areas (see Chapter 1). Even this is somewhat ambiguous, as definitions of countryside vary enormously in different regions or countries, as do the range of tourism activities and pursuits that are considered to be rural. Nevertheless, within these constraints, this broad definition represents a useful starting point for measuring the demand for rural tourism.

However, another problem of definition emerges immediately because it is necessary to consider not only *what* is rural tourism, but also *who* is a rural tourist. Again, this could be answered by simply stating that a rural tourist is an individual who participates in tourism activities in a rural setting, but this could refer as much to someone going for a short walk in the countryside for an hour or so as to someone staying for two weeks on a farm. Furthermore, in most countries, the greatest proportion of the demand for rural tourism is accounted for by the domestic tourism market (Grolleau 1987); in the UK, for example, only about 8 per cent of overseas visitors visit the countryside. Therefore, a variety of other factors, such as distance travelled or home location must also be taken into account. For example, it is justifiable to question whether or not an individual who lives in the countryside, and who participates in rural tourism activities in their locality, should be described as a tourist.

It is important, therefore, to clarify the parameters for measuring the demand for rural tourism not only by location and activity, but also on the basis of the nature of participation in general, and by the duration of visit in particular. That is, although tourism is generally considered to include both day visits and longer stays away from the places where people normally live and work, tourism statistics frequently include only figures relating to visits including at least one night away. Conversely, in many countries the greatest proportion of visits to the countryside are day visits. In the UK, for example, it has been estimated that annually about 80 million visitor nights are spent in the countryside whereas, in 1993, 637 million day visits were made to the countryside, with the average trip being 27 km and lasting three hours (CRN 1995).

The implication of this distinction is that, on the one hand, 'tourists' (i.e. those visitors who spend at least one night in the countryside) represent a minority of the total demand for rural tourism, yet individually spend relatively more per visit. On the other hand, day visitors account for the great majority of visits, yet individually spend less. At the same time, day visitors, simply as a consequence of their greater numbers, also have a much greater cumulative impact on the rural environment compared with longer stay visitors. Thus, if the total demand for rural tourism is taken to include both day visits and longer stays, then it becomes evident that the majority of visitors to the countryside bring relatively little economic benefit to local communities whilst, arguably, causing most of the problems. Therefore, the effective planning and management of rural tourism, which optimises benefits and minimises costs or negative impacts, is dependent upon the recognition that the demand for rural tourism includes both day (leisure) visits and longer (tourism) stays and the entire range of activities encompassed by both categories.

THE HISTORICAL DEVELOPMENT OF RURAL TOURISM

Rural tourism emerged as an identifiable social leisure activity in the UK and Europe during the latter half of the eighteenth century. Prior to this, rural areas had been utilised for recreational activities, but participation was largely restricted to a privileged land-owning minority. For example, in Britain during the eleventh and twelfth centuries, large areas of the countryside were set aside so that the aristocracy could indulge in hunting; the New Forest, in southern England, was created by William I in 1079 for this very purpose. However, for the majority of people, the opportunity to participate in rural tourism or, indeed, in any form of tourism, simply did not exist.

By the late 1700s, travelling for pleasure, as opposed to travel for business, religious or educational purposes, had become well established in Europe, although it was still the preserve of those who had both the time and the money to afford it. Since the early seventeenth century the sons of the aristocracy, particularly the English, had been undertaking extensive tours around Europe for anything up to three or four years. This 'Grand Tour' (see Towner 1985) was primarily intended to complete a young gentleman's education and, although longer tours took in Switzerland, Austria, Holland and Germany, the main interest of these tourists were the cultural centres of Europe.

However, towards the end of the eighteenth century the character of the Grand Tour had changed. It became 'invaded by the bourgeosie' (Turner and Ash 1975: 41) as greater numbers of tourists from an emerging middle class toured Europe and, importantly, their purpose was not education but sightseeing. Nature and landscape became the object of the tourist 'gaze' (Urry 1990a) and, influenced to a great extent by the writings of Rousseau, a widespread fear and dislike of mountainous scenery was replaced by the desire to see and experience the beauty of nature. 'Belief in the restorative effects of happily constituted scenes and an increasingly romantic orientation to aesthetic sightseeing' (Adler 1989) led many people to visit the rural and mountain areas of Europe with Switzerland, in particular, becoming a popular tourist destination. For example, William Wordsworth toured there in 1790, writing 'ten thousand times in the course of this tour have I regretted the inability of my memory to retain a more strong impression of the beautiful forms before me' (de Beers 1949: 90). Similarly, the English Lake District was transformed into an area revered by writers, poets and artists alike as the so-called Romantic Movement signified the emergence of rural tourism (see Case study 5).

However, as with all forms of tourism, the growth and development of rural tourism into a widespread social activity enjoyed by a broad section of the population (i.e. into a form of mass tourism) was dependent on three things, namely, technological advance, the availability of free time and increases in disposable income. During the nineteenth century, the development of the railways made many rural areas more accessible to greater numbers of people and the beginnings of the tourism industry facilitated the growth of rural tourism. For example, Thomas Cook took the first package tour to Switzerland in 1863 (Gilg 1991) and by the end of the century Switzerland had a thriving rural tourism industry based largely upon Alpine climbing and health cures. By the 1920s, railways enabled the development of new Swiss resorts such as Wengen and Grindelwald and further developments, including the introduction of chair lifts and cable cars, transformed the Bernese Oberland into a popular summer rural tourism destination, now attracting over half a million visitors each year (Flint 1992).

Similar patterns of rural tourism development are evident in other regions. Butler (1985), for example, traces the evolution of tourism in the Scottish Highlands. The early travellers to the area were followed, from 1810 onwards, by the 'romantic' tourists inspired, in particular, by the writings of Sir Walter Scott and, later, the paintings of Turner. The period from 1865–1914 witnessed the construction of the railway system in Scotland and the associated development of hotels and resorts then, from the early twentieth century onwards, road building and increased car ownership heralded the start of mass tourism to the Highlands. In the United States, too, the relatively wild and mountainous areas of the west were feared by early settlers but, during the nineteenth century, wilderness areas came to be viewed as places to be both preserved and also promoted for public enjoyment and recreation (Shaw and Williams 1994: 227). This led to the development of national parks in the United States from 1872 onwards and, from their earliest days, the parks proved to be a popular rural tourism resource. The current demand for rural tourism in the western state of Utah is described in the following case study.

Case study 4: Rural tourism in Utah

Covering an area of 84,990 square miles, Utah is the eleventh largest of America's 50 states and one of the 'Four Corners States', so called because it is the only part of the United States where state boundaries join at right-angles (Figure 3.1). Despite its size, however, Utah's

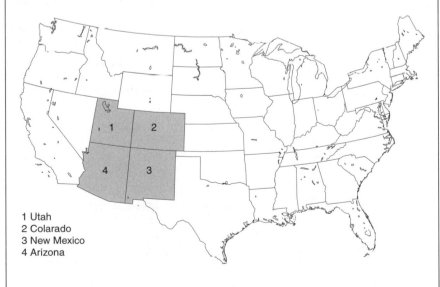

1 Utah
2 Colarado
3 New Mexico
4 Arizona

Figure 3.1 Utah and the Four Corners States

population in 1994 stood at just 1,916,000, over 80 per cent of whom live along the Wasatch Front, the valley bordering the Wasatch mountains in the northern part of the state where the capital, Salt Lake City, is located (Figure 3.2). Thus, much of Utah is sparsely populated, yet the state as a whole offers a variety of spectacular scenery and an enormous range of outdoor recreational activities.

It is not surprising, therefore, that tourism is one of the most important economic activities in Utah and also one of the fastest growing industries, outpacing the overall growth of the economy in most years. In 1994, tourism was worth an estimated $3.35 billion to the economy and supported 69,000 jobs (8 per cent of all employment) in the state (Utah 1995), figures which are likely to continue

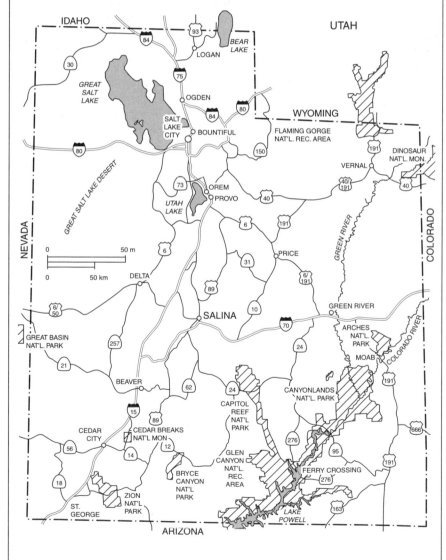

Figure 3.2 Map of Utah

to increase, particularly as Salt Lake City is hosting the Winter Olympics in 2002.

One problem, however, is to define what is *rural tourism*, as opposed to other forms of tourism, in Utah. On the one hand, it may be argued that, with the exception of visits to Salt Lake City (the major attractions there being those associated with the Church of the Latter Day Saints, the city having been founded in 1847 by the Mormon prophet Brigham Young), all tourism in Utah is, in effect, rural. On the other hand, there are certain activities, such as skiing (a major sector of Utah tourism, with almost 3 million skier visits a year to the popular centres such as Snowbird and Park City) which would not normally be associated with rural tourism although, during the summer months, the mountains attract hikers and climbers in large numbers. Here, rural tourism in Utah is taken to be all activities other than skiing.

A second difficulty is how to quantify the demand for rural tourism in the state. Geographically, the state can be divided into three areas, namely, the Basin and Range Province to the west of the state, including the Great Salt Lake Desert, the central Middle Rocky Mountain area to the north-east, and the Colorado Plateau in the south-east half of the state, where the most well-known natural attractions are located (Figure 3.2). With the exception of the latter area, most rural tourism activities are informal, occurring in the wider, unmanaged countryside and, hence, difficult to measure. For example, driving along the dirt trails which follow the old Pony Express route through the western desert regions is a popular activity, whilst the Glen Canyon National Recreation Area which includes Lake Powell, the world's second largest man-made reservoir, annually attracts almost 3 million visitors who participate in informal land and water based activities.

However, much of the demand for rural tourism in Utah is focused on the southern half of the state where the major, managed attractions are located. These include the five national parks located in Utah and four of the state's six national monuments, whilst the state as a whole boasts 45 state parks and seven national forests which cover over 9 million acres of land for recreation and exploration. Undoubtedly, it is the national parks which are the state's prime rural tourism attraction, together attracting over 5 million visits each year (Table 3.1). Total visits to the National Parks have grown at 3.7 per cent annually, roughly reflecting the growth in the number of out-of-state visitors to Utah. However, the apparent fall in visitor numbers during 1994 resulted from a change in the basis of calculating the figures rather than a measured decrease.

Collectively, the state parks receive almost 7 million visits annually although individually they are, generally, less popular than the national parks, the exceptions being Great Salt Lake State Park and Willard Bay State Park which, owing to their proximity to the main centres of population, together attract over 1 million visits each year.

No figures exist for participation levels in different rural tourism activities in Utah. However, car touring, off-highway 4-wheel driving,

Table 3.1 Visits to Utah national parks

	Visits ('000s)				
	1990	*1991*	*1992*	*1993*	*1994*
Arches N.P.	620.7	705.9	799.8	773.7	777.2
Bryce Canyon N.P.	862.7	929.1	1018.0	1108.0	1028.1
Canyonlands N.P.	276.8	339.3	395.7	434.8	429.9
Capitol Reef N.P.	562.5	618.1	675.8	660.8	605.3
Zion N.P.	2102.4	2237.0	2390.6	2414.5	2270.9
Total	4425.1	4829.4	5280.1	5391.8	5111.4

Source: Adapted from Utah (1995)

camping and hiking, cycling, hunting and fishing (there are over 1,000 fishable lakes in the state), snowmobiling, and a variety of water sports, including sailing and white-water rafting, are all popular. Much of this demand is accounted for by local visitors who reside within Utah, but over 15 million visits were made by out-of-state tourists in 1994. Interestingly, of these, fewer than 900,000 were overseas visitors. Nevertheless, the state's tourism accommodation sector achieves over 70 per cent average occupancy levels which, given the fact that tourism in Utah is largely rural in nature, demonstrates the importance of the sector to the overall state economy.

Despite its development during the nineteenth century, it was not until the twentieth century that rural tourism became a widely enjoyed activity. Indeed, it is the twentieth century that has seen not only a rapid growth in the demand for rural tourism but also increasing diversity in the range of rural activities and pursuits. In the period between the two World Wars many people enjoyed paid holidays for the first time and, with improvements in transport and mobility, the countryside became increasingly accessible. In the UK, activities such as rambling, cycling and fishing became popular during this period and there were growing demands for access to the wider countryside, much of which was privately owned and off-limits to the increasing numbers of visitors (Hill 1980). Elsewhere in Europe, participation in rural tourism increased as a result of people who had migrated into towns and cities being able to return to the countryside to stay with friends or relatives or to spend their holidays in 'the modest second homes they have inherited' (Cavaco 1995: 129). This, in part, led to the long-standing tradition of rural tourism based on farm accommodation in a number of countries, including Switzerland, Austria, Sweden and Germany. Importantly, during this period, it was generally the less affluent members of society who participated in rural tourism in their own countries whilst the better off were starting to enjoy regular overseas tourism.

The major growth in demand has occurred since 1945. Of course, this is the same period that has witnessed the dramatic growth of tourism in general, and mass international tourism in particular, and the increase in demand for rural tourism to some extent has reflected this broader development of tourism. However, the most influential factor in terms of rural tourism has been the rapid increase in car ownership; in the UK there were 2 million cars on the roads in 1939, a figure which had risen to over 22 million by the 1990s. Combined with increasing prosperity and greater amounts of free time in most industrialised countries, more people were able to visit the countryside in greater numbers and it has been estimated, for example, that the number of day trips to the countryside on a typical summer weekend in the UK doubled between 1968 and 1977 (Harrison 1991).

In more recent years, the overall demand for rural tourism has levelled off in many countries, although the range of activities and types of rural holidays has continued to expand. This is attributable to a number of factors, but primarily the increase in demand for overseas holidays has reduced the demand for traditional, rural-based holidays; during the 1980s, for example, the number of overseas visits made by UK residents increased by 70 per cent. However, the emergence of new tourism products, such as inland all-weather resorts, which have become increasingly popular in northern Europe, and city-based tourism, have also had an impact on the level of demand for rural tourism.

Conversely, in the face of this competition, it is possible to identify a number of reasons why the demand for rural tourism has been maintained:

- In most industrialised countries, increases in available leisure time have resulted in the growth of short breaks and the second or third holiday market. Many holidays of this kind are taken in rural areas.
- Since the early 1980s, greater interest in heritage in general and the development of the 'heritage industry' (Hewison 1987) in particular has resulted in growing interest in rural areas which, in many countries, are considered to be representative of a nation's 'true' heritage.
- Health concerns and increased awareness of the benefits of a healthy lifestyle have encouraged participation in a variety of activities which, by their nature, occur in a rural setting.
- Improvements in the quality and availability of outdoor clothing and equipment and the image status of, for example, all-terrain bicycles or 4-wheel drive vehicles have made it easier for many people to enjoy recreation in the countryside.
- Rural agencies, tourist boards and private sector organisations have been increasingly promoting the development of rural tourism and marketing it to both domestic and international visitors.

Some of these issues will be considered in greater detail later in this chapter but, generally, as the level of demand for rural tourism has changed, so too has the nature of that demand. It has become more diversified as a result of the 'rediscovery' of the countryside by the middle and upper classes (Cavaco 1995) and, therefore, the use of the countryside for tourism has become inextricably linked with broader issues, such as environmental concerns and the role of the countryside as the antithesis to

modern life and, implicitly, modern, mass tourism. It is important, therefore, to examine those factors which determine or influence not only the
total demand for rural tourism, but also the characteristics of that demand.

RURAL TOURISM: DEMAND FACTORS

There is no doubt that rural tourism represents a significant sector of the
overall demand for tourism, although it has been noted that precise quantitative data about the size of the rural tourism market are lacking (OECD
1994). A number of reasons may be put forward for this apparent gap in
the tourism statistics, such as lack of agreement about what actually constitutes rural tourism, but, as suggested earlier, it is the very nature of rural
tourism that renders exact measurement of demand an impossible task.
Nevertheless, attempts have been made to estimate the overall demand for
rural tourism, such as in England and Wales where studies have shown
that, over an average year, over three-quarters of the adult population visit
the countryside at some time (Countryside Commission 1995a). In
Europe, a survey of tourism behaviour in member states was undertaken
in the mid-1980s and this, too, demonstrated the relative importance of the
countryside as a tourist destination. Overall, it was found that 25 per cent
of Europeans spent their holidays in the countryside, a figure which rises
to 48 per cent if the category of 'mountains' is also included as rural
(Table 3.2).

The European statistics are not directly comparable owing to differences in the meaning of countryside in different countries, whilst
geographical and socio-economic variations also influence tourism preferences. Furthermore, the figures presented here refer only to main holidays
and do not include second/third holidays, short breaks or day trips which
together account for the greater proportion of the demand for rural
tourism. Perhaps not surprisingly, the overwhelming preference for main
holidays is the seaside (52 per cent for the EU) but, interestingly, 29 per

Table 3.2 European holiday destinations (per cent)

Country	Countryside	Mountains	Cities	Seaside
Belgium	25	19	5	55
Denmark	35	14	40	42
W. Germany	34	30	15	44
Greece	8	11	20	70
Spain	27	19	27	53
France	29	27	18	51
Ireland	27	8	37	46
Italy	11	24	19	58
Luxembourg	19	29	17	62
Netherlands	39	32	21	36
Portugal	29	8	24	62
UK	29	13	19	58
EU	**25**	**23**	**19**	**52**

Source: Grolleau (1987)

cent of Europeans prefer the countryside for their second holidays, 23 per cent prefer mountainous areas, 25 per cent the cities and 29 per cent the seaside. This evidence tends to support the argument that the demand for rural tourism has been sustained by increases in the availability of leisure time and levels of income, manifested in the growth in short breaks and additional holidays.

Evidence pointing to the relative popularity of rural tourism can also be found in other tourism statistics, such as participation in special interest or acotourism, but these overall figures, although demonstrating the importance and strength of the rural tourism market, conceal some important characteristics of demand. In other words, overall demand figures reveal little about who visits the countryside, how frequently, and what they do when they are there, facts which are essential to all planners and managers of rural tourism. For example, it is widely claimed that rural tourism has become a middle-class activity (Harrison 1991; Cavaco 1995) and surveys have shown that, in general, both the domestic and international rural holiday markets comprise the more affluent and better educated sectors of society. Therefore, it is necessary to examine the demand for rural tourism in much greater detail.

Characteristics of demand

Relatively little research has been undertaken into the characteristics of the demand for rural tourism, although a comprehensive survey of tourism in the UK countryside was undertaken during the 1980s (Countryside Commission 1985) which, along with more recent follow-up surveys, provides an in-depth examination of factors determining the demand for rural tourism in the UK. These factors may not, of course, be directly comparable to the demand for rural tourism in other countries; however, other studies do suggest that similar characteristics and motivational factors are generally applicable.

In general, the surveys have shown that participation in rural tourism in the UK has remained reasonably static since the 1980s, although there has been a downward trend in the figures (Table 3.3). During an average summer month about half the UK population visit the countryside, typically making three or four visits, with both the proportion of the population going to the countryside and the average number of visits

Table 3.3 Proportion of people visiting the countryside (per cent)

Month	1984	1985	1986	1987	1988	1989
February	44	37	34	37	36	43
May	59	56	52	51	N/A	52
June	61	56	58	54	57	52
July	70	55	60	53	59	53
August	69	62	59	56	60	51
October	54	44	41	40	44	37
Monthly Average	60	52	51	49	51	48

Source: Countryside Commission (1990a)

showing some decline since 1984 (a hot summer in 1984 led to a higher than average participation in rural tourism). However, a more significant decline has been experienced in the number of tourist nights spent in the countryside. In 1984, 118 million visitor nights were spent in the countryside; by 1990, the figure was 81 million, the fall being attributable to both the changing demand for rural recreation and the recession of the late 1980s (Curry 1994: 89).

Of greater importance, the surveys show that, although a large proportion of the population visit the countryside at least once during a year, the great majority of visits to the countryside are in fact made by a relatively small section of the population (Table 3.4). In 1984, the 17 per cent of the population who were frequent visitors to the countryside (nine or more visits in a typical four week period) accounted for 68 per cent of all visits; by 1990, 11 per cent of the population made 61 per cent of all visits. At the other end of the scale, half of the UK population do not visit the countryside during a typical four week period.

Thus, although rural tourism in the UK appears to be a popular activity in terms of overall demand, the surveys show that not only is the countryside attracting fewer visitors each year but also that rural recreation is, in one sense, a minority activity. Indeed, in 1990, 80 per cent of visits were made by 20 per cent of the population. The implication of these figures is, of course, that rural tourism may not be the economic panacea to the problems facing rural areas (see Chapter 2), particularly if an increasing number of businesses are seeking a share of a shrinking market.

Influences on demand

There is an enormous variety of factors that, at the individual level, influence the demand for rural tourism. For example, the availability of time or income, family constraints and more general factors, such as attitude to the countryside or the attraction of other forms of tourism, are just some of the potential influences on demand. At the same time, as Curry (1994: 92) points out, many of the factors that are considered to 'trigger' participation in rural tourism are increasing, yet participation is falling. Therefore, it would appear to be a difficult task to identify general influences on demand.

Table 3.4 Share of visits to the countryside (per cent)

Trips in average four week period	1984	1985	1986	1990
No visits	40	48	49	50
1 visit	11	10	10	12
2–4 visits	20	19	19	18
5–8 visits	12	10	10	9
9+ visits	17	13	12	11

Source: Countryside Commission (1985; 1995a)

Nevertheless, there are certain dominant influences on the demand for rural tourism.

- *Car ownership* – the 1984 survey in the UK found that people owning or having use of a car were three times more likely to visit the countryside than those with no car available to them. Indeed, over 80 per cent of all visits to the countryside are made by car whilst in popular areas, such as some national parks, the figure is over 90 per cent of visits. Conversely, it was found that only 5 per cent of visits were made by public transport. Thus, in other countries with a higher level of car ownership than in the UK, such as Germany or the United States, it is likely that most, if not all, visits to the countryside will be dependent on the use of a car. This has important implications for the management of the countryside, particularly within the context of environmental protection, and in some areas, such as national parks in the United States and in the UK, methods of limiting access by car are currently under consideration.
- *Social background* – It is widely believed that the demand for rural tourism is socially classified. That is, although participation is spread across all social groups in society, that spread of participation is seen to be uneven (Curry 1994) and the evidence from surveys certainly confirms this. For example, Fitton (1979) found that people in professional or managerial positions are three times more likely to visit the countryside than those who are unemployed or on minimum incomes, whilst more recent studies demonstrate the correlation between social class and participation in rural tourism (Table 3.5). In 1990, the 42 per cent of the UK population who were ABC1s made 52 per cent of visits to the countryside (Countryside Commission 1995a: 4). This group also tends to visit the countryside more frequently whereas, perhaps not surprisingly, people who are unemployed or on low incomes make a disproportionately low number of visits.

  The income associated with employment in the upper half of the social spectrum is undoubtedly a relevant factor, whilst education and knowledge of the countryside are also related and may also, therefore, influence demand. However, social background is also of particular relevance when considering the demand for specific rural tourism activities. For example, fishing is most popular amongst skilled manual workers whilst

Table 3.5 Countryside visits and social class

Social Class	Percentage of population		Percentage of visits	
	1984	*1990*	*1984*	*1990*
A	2	2	2	2
B	13	13	20	19
C1	23	27	28	31
C2	27	29	27	28
D/E	28	9	19	8
D/E (unemployed)	7	20	4	12

Source: Countryside Commission (1985; 1995a)

the lower classes have been found to prefer commercialised, 'collective' (Urry 1990b) sites or destinations, such as country pubs or safari parks; see Curry (1994) for details and also Walter (1982).

- *Housing location* – Where people live is also a distinctive factor in the demand for rural tourism. In 1990, it was found that those people who live in or close to the countryside (within one to three miles) are more likely to visit the countryside and to be frequent visitors than those who live further away (Countryside Commission 1995a). This mirrors earlier surveys which suggested that those who live in affluent suburbs and modern family housing are more likely to participate in rural tourism than inner city residents.

There are, of course, a variety of other factors that influence the demand for rural tourism. Both age and gender reflect upon the frequency of visits to the countryside, whilst some have also identified membership of clubs or organisations with rural links, such as sports or conservation bodies, as a positive influence on participation. Other more general influences may also be suggested. For example, the weather has a direct influence on the level of demand, as does the increasing interest in home-based leisure activities. Overall, however, the 'typical' rural tourist is *more likely* to be younger, more affluent, in professional or managerial employment, a car owner and living in or near the countryside. These factors are largely inter-related but, nevertheless, tend to confirm that rural tourism is typically a more middle-class activity.

RURAL TOURISM: MOTIVATION FACTORS

The influences on demand described above are, essentially, factors which enable people to participate in rural tourism. They do not, however, explain *why* people wish to do so. The countryside is one of many different tourist destinations and, therefore, it is important to consider why people choose to visit the countryside or what it is about the countryside that attracts tourists in the first place. In other words, the successful development of rural tourism is dependent on an understanding of what motivates people to visit the countryside.

All tourist behaviour or activity results from motivation. It is the 'trigger that sets off all events in travel' (Parrinello 1993) and, as such, is the very basis of the demand for tourism. Therefore, the analysis of motivational factors can help explain travel behaviour and destination choice and, in a practical sense, enable tourism organisations to satisfy the needs of tourists. Motivation in the context of the demand for tourism is considered in detail elsewhere (see, for example, Dann 1981; Ryan 1991; Mansfeld 1992; Sharpley 1994) but, generally, it can be seen as comprising two sets of factors.

- *Push factors* – Also described as 'person-specific' factors (Goodall 1991), push factors are those which influence or push an individual into deciding upon a particular form of tourism or, indeed, into purchasing a holiday as opposed to another product. They may result from personal, psychological needs or from broader influences but, more often than not, push factors are collectively described as simply the need to escape.

● *Pull factors* – These relate to the characteristics or attributes of particular destinations or sites and are the factors which determine destination choice once the decision to participate in tourism has been made. Thus, 'destination-specific' attributes are those which pull tourists to particular destinations and which best satisfy tourists' needs within the constraints of distance, costs and so on.

The motivational factors influencing the demand for rural tourism can be linked to both push and pull factors and, frequently, the distinction between the two is indistinct. For example, certain activities, such as hiking or rambling, implicitly depend upon a rural setting but, for the tourist, the need to experience the peace and quiet of the rural environment may be as important, if not more so, than simply having countryside to hike in. Conversely, it may simply be a particular activity that attracts visitors to the countryside. Therefore, the reasons for visiting the countryside can be considered from two perspectives, namely, how the countryside is used (motivation by purpose) and the broader attractions of the rural environment.

Activities in the countryside

Reference has already been made to the diverse range of touristic activities that occur in the rural setting (see Chapter 1). However, the level of participation in different activities can also serve as an indication of why people visit the countryside, as evidenced by surveys in the UK. The Countryside Commission (1995a) lists eighteen different activities which may be defined as purposes for visiting the countryside (Table 3.6).

What is important, however, is not the range of activities itself, but the relative popularity of each. For example, at least half the UK population go on a drive or outing in the countryside each year, whereas less than 5 per cent of people participate in organised conservation work or horse riding, hunting and shooting.

Table 3.7 indicates the level of participation in the main countryside activities over a year.

The implication of these figures is that the majority of visits to the countryside are for informal, unplanned activities. Indeed, three times as many visits are made to the open countryside as to specific, managed sites or destinations. This suggests that the majority of visitors to the countryside are motivated not by the opportunity to participate in a particular activity but by the broader attractions of the rural environment, a notion that is confirmed by research into visitors' motivations for visiting the countryside.

Table 3.6 Countryside activities

- Visiting the seas, coast or cliff tops (but not seaside resorts)
- Visiting historic buildings, stately homes, museums, gardens or parks in the countryside (excluding country parks)
- Visiting country parks
- Visiting zoos, safari or wildlife parks in the countryside
- Visiting nature reserves in the countryside
- Drives, outings, picnics, etc. in the countryside (including visits to attractive villages)
- Long walks, hikes or rambles of at least 2 miles [3.2 km] (round trip) in the countryside, either from car or home
- Bird watching/nature study in the countryside
- Fishing in the countryside
- Horse riding or pony trekking in the countryside
- Shooting in the countryside
- Hunting in the countryside
- Taking active part in other organised sport (e.g. football, cricket, cycling, golf, sailing, running, climbing, motor sport) in the countryside
- Taking active part in other informal sport (e.g. jogging, kicking a ball about, beach games, throwing frisbees) in the countryside
- Watching any organised sport in the countryside (in person, not on TV)
- Visiting friends or relatives in the countryside
- Carrying out any organised conservation or recreation work in the countryside (e.g. tree planting, clearing of footpaths)
- 'Picking your own '(fruit, vegetables) in the countryside

Table 3.7 Participation in activities in the countryside

Activity	Percentage of Population
Drive/outing/picnic	56
Visit friends or relatives	40
Visit the seas/coast	39
Visit an historic site	39
Long walk	33
Active sport	31
Visit a country park	30
Informal sport	25

Source: Countryside Commission (1995a)

Attractions of the rural environment

As with the demand for rural tourism as a whole, there is a lack of research into what attracts people to the countryside. At the same time, both the spontaneous nature of much of the demand for rural tourism and also the potentially different meaning and importance of the countryside and rural tourism in different countries and regions make it difficult, if not impossible, to formulate a set of motivations based upon the attractions of the rural environment. Nevertheless, qualitative research both in the UK and elsewhere demonstrate that the rural environment in general is the prime attraction of the countryside. For example, the National Countryside Recreation Survey in the UK found that well over half of all visits to the countryside were made specifically because of the rural environment (Table 3.8).

Table 3.8 Motivation for last trip from home to the countryside

Motivation	Percentage of trips
Wanted to go to that particular place	29
Wanted to go somewhere in the countryside	28
Wanted to take part in that particular activity	19
To be with family	10
Other reasons	14

Source: Countryside Commission (1985)

Other studies in the UK have confirmed that most visitors to the countryside are attracted by its intrinsic qualities, the sense of space and freedom and the opportunity it offers for peace and relaxation, with over 80 per cent visiting the countryside because it is quiet and peaceful (Countryside Commission 1987b). Similarly, Harrison *et al.* (1986) found that the appeal of the countryside lies in the contrast it offers to modern, urban living, in particular in terms of the sights, sounds and smells of the rural environment. However, in both cases, it is not clear whether the desired attributes of the rural environment are based upon prior experience or perceptions resulting from the social construction of the countryside as discussed in Chapter 1. Moreover, it is accepted that literary or cultural associations are a significant influence on the demand for rural tourism; Brontë's Yorkshire, Hardy's Dorset and Wordsworth's Lake District are all rural areas in England which have benefited in a tourism sense from famous literary links (Squire 1994), whilst popular television programmes have also led to a growth in tourism in what are, in effect, fictitious rural areas.

In Europe, the results of various surveys into both general or sector specific aspects of rural tourism tend to mirror the UK findings. For example, the Dutch, who particularly favour the countryside as a tourist destination, list natural sites to visit and unspoilt scenery as the most important attributes of destination areas. In Germany and Italy, research has been undertaken specifically into farm tourism, with similar results. In Germany, where there is a long tradition of farm tourism, the principal motivations for visiting the countryside are to discover nature (76 per cent of visitors) and to enjoy affordable family holidays in a different, calm environment. In Italy, the need for peace and quiet, nature and scenery were the dominant motivations for choosing farm holidays (see Grolleau 1987 and Cavaco 1995 for more detail).

Overall, then, the limited research into the motivation for visiting the countryside would suggest that the majority of visitors are seeking the actual or perceived attributes of the rural environment, such as peace and tranquillity, a sense of space and freedom, and authenticity and tradition, factors which collectively represent the antithesis to modern, urban life. This is not to say, of course, that people do not visit the countryside for specific purposes or activities, or that formal, managed sites do not attract visitors. For example, entrance to, and activities within, many US national parks are strictly controlled and managed, yet they are increasingly popular tourist destinations. Similarly, National Trust properties in England

and Wales, the majority of which are in rural areas, attract over 11 million visitors each year. Nevertheless, for the majority, visiting the countryside is a spontaneous activity based upon the desire to experience rurality in its broadest sense and thus, there are important implications for the development of tourism and visitor management in rural areas.

Many of the points raised in his chapter are usefully summarised in the following case study on the demand for tourism in the English Lake District.

Case study 5: Tourism in the Lake District

For more than two centuries the Lake District, lying in the north west of England (Figure 3.3) has attracted visitors from home and abroad. One of the earliest known visitors was the poet Thomas Gray who undertook a ten-day excursion in the area in 1769 (and, according to Rollinson (1967), is now widely regarded as the first genuine 'tourist') and, during the late eighteenth and early nineteenth centuries, the Lake

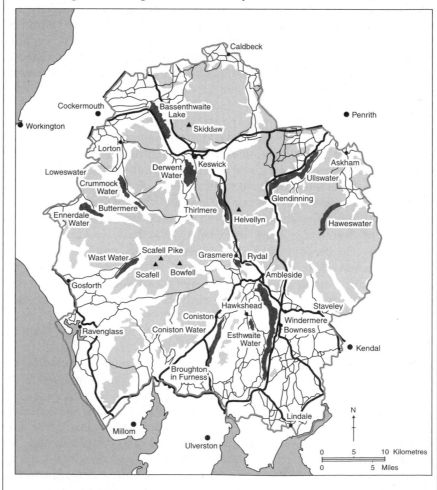

Figure 3.3 The English Lake District

District became increasingly popularised by the work of the 'Romantics', such as Wordsworth, Keats and Shelley, as well as the paintings of Turner, Constable and Gainsborough.

However, it was the arrival of the railways in 1847 that set the scene for present day rural tourism in the Lake District. The railhead towns of Windermere, Coniston and Keswick grew rapidly as the area became accessible to day trippers from the northern industrial towns and, for example, over 10,000 people visited Windermere on Whit Monday in 1883 (Berry and Beard 1980). This signalled the beginning of the Lake District's reputation as a major holiday destination, the importance of which grew from the 1950s onwards (the Lake District was designated a National Park in 1951) with the rapid increases in leisure time, disposable income and, in particular, car ownership. These factors, combined with the construction of new motorways, have brought an estimated 20 million people within a three-hour drive of the Lake District (Jones 1990).

The area is today one of the most popular rural tourist destinations in the UK and, after the Peak District, the second most visited national park in the country. There is also no doubting the importance of tourism to the economy of Lakeland. Although estimates vary, between 12 and 18 million people visit the National Park each year with annual tourism receipts in the county of Cumbria as a whole amounting to £542 million in 1994 (ETB/CTB 1995). Of this, 78 per cent is generated by domestic tourists staying at least one night in the region, 12 per cent by domestic day visitors and 10 per cent by overseas visitors. Not surprisingly, tourism also supports a significant proportion of total employment and, as jobs in traditional Lakeland industries have been lost (for example, jobs in farming fell by 9 per cent between 1977 and 1984, one of the periods of greatest decline), the importance of tourism-related employment has increased. In some parts of the Lake District as many as 75 per cent of jobs are dependent on tourism (Bingham 1988) whilst, in the National Park as a whole, over one third of all employment is tourism related.

Thus, tourism brings significant benefits to the Lake District, but it also causes a number of negative impacts (see Chapter 2) which result from the nature of the demand for tourism in the area. In particular:

● With a nine-fold increase in private car ownership in the UK since 1950, the great majority of visitors to the Lake District arrive by car. In 1989, 79 per cent of all visits were made by car; in 1994 the figure had risen to 85 per cent (ETB/CTB 1995).
● Although tourism in Cumbria and the Lake District is dependent to a great extent on the short- and long- stay markets, less than a quarter of visitors to the National Park actually stay for one or more nights. This dominance of the day-visitor market can be explained in part by the ease of road access to the area and the fact that almost half of all visitors come from the northern half of

England, but it also mirrors general trends in the demand for rural tourism.

- Despite representing the largest market, day visitors account for just 12 per cent of tourism spending in Cumbria. Thus, the largest group of visitors brings the least economic benefit to the area but, arguably, causes the greatest impact.
- Hiking and rambling are the most popular activities and most surveys have shown that other informal activities, such as having picnics, admiring the view or visiting shops and cafes, are also popular. A number of specific visitor attractions also draw substantial numbers of visitors, including (with 1994 visitor figures) the Cumberland Pencil Museum (89,265), Dove Cottage and the Wordsworth Museum (78,484), Hill Top (the home of Beatrix Potter) (77,337), and the National Park Visitor Centre (150,000). The lakes themselves are, of course, important attractions; on the largest lake, Windermere, there were 12,500 registered power boats in 1987 and in 1994, over half a million visitors were passengers on the pleasure steamers on the lake.
- Finally, the Lake District has been found to appeal mainly to young to middle-aged people (66 per cent of visitors in 1994 were between 15 and 54 years old) and the higher social groups (ETB/CTB 1995).

Based upon these identified patterns of demand, the challenge facing tourism planners in the Lake District is to optimise the benefits of tourism and to maintain its appeal to visitors, especially those staying for short and longer holidays, whilst minimising both the negative impacts on the environment and the disruption caused to local communities. Suggested policies have included the positive promotion of the 'honeypot' tourist centres, such as Windermere and Ambleside, to counter the further spread of tourism throughout the area, the restriction of developments in sensitive areas to maintain the special appeal of the quieter and more remote parts of the lakes and fells, measures to reduce non-essential or non-local traffic throughout the National Park, and the promotion of lesser known, relatively under-utilised destinations and attractions outside the National Park boundaries.

CONCLUSION

During the nineteenth and twentieth centuries, rural tourism has emerged and developed into a separate, identifiable sector of the overall market for tourism with the corresponding growth in the demand resulting, as with all forms of tourism, primarily from greater accessibility and mobility and increases in income and free time. However, the nature of that demand has undergone a transformation as the countryside has faced increasing competition from new tourist destinations and attractions. In particular, rural tourism, although generally appealing to a wide market, has become identified with an increasingly up-market and more affluent clientele, and surveys have revealed a number of important characteristics of demand.

- Domestic day visitors account for a large proportion of the demand for rural tourism, with the great majority of visits being made by a relatively small section of the population.
- Most visitors travel to the countryside by car and participate in spontaneous, informal activities. Managed, formal sites and destinations, though popular in terms of visitor numbers, attract a relatively small proportion of total countryside visits.
- Many tourists are motivated to visit the countryside by the desire to experience the broader rural environment rather than to participate in specific activities. Therefore, actual or perceived 'rurality' as the antithesis to modern, urban life is an important element of the rural tourism experience.

Taken together, these characteristics have important implications for the development of rural tourism. In particular, there is a limit to the potential demand for rural tourism products, suggesting that rural tourism cannot be a universally successful form of economic diversification, whilst tourists' desire to experience traditional rurality means that careful planning is necessary in terms of both the supply of rural tourism and also the broader development of the countryside as a whole. Thus, the demand for and success of rural tourism is inextricably linked with the wider development and conservation of the rural resource.

QUESTIONS

1. What are the main difficulties associated with the collection and analysis of quantitative data measuring the demand for rural tourism?
2. What evidence is there to support the argument that the demand for rural tourism is socially defined?
3. Consider the main characteristics of the demand for rural tourism.
4. Why do people visit the countryside?

FURTHER READING

Curry, N. (1994) *Countryside Recreation, Access and Land Use Planning*, London: E & FN Spon (especially Chapter 4).

Grolleau, H. (1987) *Rural Tourism in the 12 Member States of the European Economic Community*, Paris: TER.

Harrison, C. (1991) *Countryside Recreation in a Changing Society*, London: TMS Partnership.

Johnson, P. and Thomas, B. (1992) *Choice and Demand in Tourism*, London: Mansell.

Sharpley, R. (1996) *Tourism and Leisure in the Countryside,* 2nd edition, Huntingdon: Elm Publications.

4 The supply of rural tourism

INTRODUCTION

It has already been demonstrated that the demand for rural tourism encompasses an enormous variety of activities which occur in an equally large variety of locations. It is not surprising, therefore, that the supply of rural tourism is equally diverse. It involves a multitude of organisations and businesses, some private and some public, ranging from large, national companies to small, family-run concerns, which collectively provide an enormous array of products and services to visitors in rural areas.

However, although the demand for and supply of rural tourism are, in effect, two sides of the rural tourism coin, there is 'no simple interface' (Glyptis 1991: 125) between the two. In other words, the overall provision of rural tourism is a complex process, made all the more difficult, perhaps, by the need to integrate tourism within the broader planning and development of rural areas and, as a result, the supply of rural tourism is usually considered from the perspective of individual sectors or areas of activity that together comprise the overall rural tourism 'product'. It is not unusual, for example, for studies to be undertaken into particular market segments, such as the agritourism market, into the provision of opportunities for specific activities, such as mountain-biking, or into the effectiveness of certain supply policies, such as the designation of national parks as a means of reconciling conservation with recreation.

Whilst the importance of these specific, micro studies cannot be denied, it is also essential, however, to consider the supply of rural tourism from a macro perspective. In other words, from the point of view of the tourist, the overall rural tourism 'product' comprises more than just, for example, accommodation facilities, attractions and, perhaps, the ability to undertake a variety of different activities. As discussed in Chapter 3, many people are motivated to visit the countryside because of its intrinsic rural qualities. The sense of space, the opportunity to enjoy the peace and tranquillity of the countryside, and the physical and cultural characteristics of the rural environment are also important elements of the rural tourism experience and part of the overall tourism 'product'. Furthermore, other factors, such as transport or ease of access, have a bearing on the enjoyment or satisfaction gained from a visit to the countryside and, therefore, an understanding of the inter-dependency of these different aspects is of fundamental importance.

The purpose of this chapter is to explore these diverse elements of the supply of rural tourism. For convenience, although somewhat artificially, the roles and activities of the public and private sectors are considered separately and, given the enormous range of attractions, facilities and activities that comprise the supply of rural tourism, as well as a variety of related issues, such as the role of national parks, it is only possible to present a broad and introductory overview of the subject. Nevertheless, the main theme throughout the chapter is the need to recognise the characteristics and constituents of the total rural tourism product and it is first necessary, therefore, to consider this in more detail.

THE TOTAL RURAL TOURISM PRODUCT

All tourist visits or experiences are comprised of a number of different products or elements. Typically, these elements include transport, accommodation, entertainment, attractions, and retail and refreshment facilities and, together, they represent the supply of tourism. Sometimes these various elements are organised and sold as a package by tour operators or travel agents, either as an 'off the shelf' holiday or as an individually designed trip, sometimes tourists themselves select and combine the various elements. In either case, however, these elements collectively 'produce an amalgam of activities and functions called a *tourist product*' (Murphy 1985: 14).

There are two ways of considering the tourism product. On the one hand, it may be viewed from the point of view of the tourism industry, or the producers of the tourism product, an approach which tends to concentrate on the problems and challenges facing particular sectors. Farm tourism, for example, is currently the focus of much attention throughout Europe, whilst individual operators or industry sectors, perhaps inevitably, consider the supply of tourism and potential markets from their own perspective. Thus, the development and promotion of inland resorts, such as the Center Parcs holiday villages, are promoted as an up-market and environmentally friendly form of rural tourism but are, essentially, a successful business venture.

On the other hand, the tourism product can be viewed from the point of view of the tourist. In this case, the tourism product becomes the entire tourism experience and, in a sense, the tourism product then becomes greater than the sum of its parts. In other words, the rural tourism product is not simply a collection of attractions, facilities and recreational opportunities in the countryside but the total experience which, frequently, includes periods or phases both prior to and following the actual visit to the countryside. In an early work, Clawson and Knetsch (1966) suggested that outdoor recreational experiences are made up of five separate and identifiable phases or stages:

- The *anticipation* stage, when a visit or holiday is planned. This may often be the most satisfying or pleasurable part of the tourism experience and is of direct relevance to perceptions of the countryside as a destination. The anticipation stage may cover a long period, as when planning a long or main holiday, or it may be fleeting or momentary when a spontaneous decision is made to visit the countryside.

- The *travel to site* stage, which is an implicit element of any tourism experience. In some cases this stage may be considered to be something to be endured rather than enjoyed and, therefore, ease of access becomes an important factor. In other cases, however, the journey to the destination may be part of the purpose of a trip; for example, opportunities for sightseeing on the journey may be as important as the stay at the destination itself.

- The *on-site experience* stage, which is usually the most important part of a visit. The quality and range of attractions, the availability, cost and quality of facilities, the range of recreational opportunities and even the extent to which the visit satisfies or matches perceptions and expectations are all elements of the on-site experience and, to a great extent, determine the overall success of a visit or holiday.

- The *return travel home* stage. At this stage of a visit or holiday, tourists are usually anxious to return home as easily as possible, although circular routes based upon sightseeing opportunities may be planned elements of a trip. Conversely, problems on the return trip, such as long delays or traffic jams, may potentially diminish the overall satisfaction of the tourism experience.

- The *recollection* stage is a frequently overlooked but, nevertheless, vital part of the tourism experience. Memories of holidays are important, not only because they prolong the experience but also because they form the basis for anticipating the next trip. Indeed, it may be difficult to differentiate between recollection and anticipation, and tourism may then be seen as a cyclical process whereby each tourism experience merges into the next.

If these five stages are applied to rural tourism, it is evident that the rural tourism product comprises much more than, for example, accommodation facilities and the ability to participate in certain activities. The journey to and from the destination, the extent to which perceptions of 'rurality' (see Chapter 1) are verified or satisfied and the resulting memories of a trip are all elements of the product. Thus, the tourism product may be seen as a 'bundle or package of tangible and intangible components' (Middleton 1988: 79), including destination attractions and facilities, accessibility, image and price, which combine to form the overall experience (see Figure 4.1).

It is also evident that these separate components are inter-dependent and that a tourist's dissatisfaction with one component may spoil or diminish the overall tourism experience. For example, the enjoyment of a visit to the countryside may be marred by anything from traffic jams on the way home or high prices for food and drink to the sight of

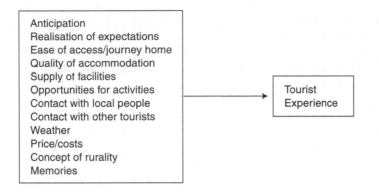

Figure 4.1 Elements of the total tourism experience

large groups of people enjoying the 'solitude' of a hike in the mountains or the perceived intrusion of modern technology in a traditional rural landscape.

The major implication of this total product perspective on the supply of rural tourism is that, whilst the problems and challenges facing individual sectors or components are important within themselves, they should be considered not in isolation but within the broader context of the overall tourist experience. As discussed in Chapter 5, this is of particular relevance to the marketing of rural tourism, but it also highlights the need to recognise not only the inter-dependency of the diverse elements of the rural tourism product but also the links between the supply of rural tourism and more general planning and management of the countryside as a whole.

WHO SUPPLIES RURAL TOURISM?

It is generally accepted that 'tourist development in rural regions is characterized by a multiplicity of small-scale, independent developers' (Pearce 1989: 77) and, therefore, it would seem logical to suggest that, by and large, rural tourism is supplied by a large number of smaller organisations within the private sector. In the context of the rural tourism industry, this is normally the case. In most countries, accommodation, attractions, restaurants and other facilities in rural areas are usually small-scale private businesses and, particularly when compared with other sectors of the overall tourism market, rural tourism has relatively few large-scale operators, although there are exceptions. In the UK, for example, the Rank Organisation is currently developing its 'Oasis Village' inland resorts in rural areas to compete with Center Parcs whilst Thomson Holidays, the country's largest international tour operator, now dominates the supply of countryside holiday cottages.

However, private tourism businesses represent only part of the supply of rural tourism. The rural environment itself is an essential element of the rural tourism product and, hence, also part of the supply of rural tourism. In some instances, rural areas that are particularly popular as tourism destinations and worthy of protection may be owned and managed by the state, most commonly as national parks. In other instances, national or local governments may not actually own land in popular tourist areas but, nevertheless, strive to provide and maintain opportunities for rural recreational activities, such as ensuring access over private land, through legislation and other controls. Similarly, government policies in related areas, such as agriculture, transport, planning and conservation, also directly influence tourism development and, therefore, the public sector, both locally and nationally, has an important role to play in the supply of rural tourism.

It is important to point out that, in addition to the private and public sectors, the voluntary sector is also involved in the supply of rural tourism. This may arise through the ownership of land or buildings by conservation organisations, through the supply of accommodation facilities by, for example, the Youth Hostel Association, or through the provision of conservation or environmental holidays sold by non-profit tourism organisations. One of the largest providers of rural tourism opportunities within the voluntary sector, certainly within Europe if not globally, is the National Trust in the UK. As a conservation organisation with over two million members, the National Trust owns almost 240,000 hectares of countryside in England, Wales and Northern Ireland, much of which is open to public access, as well as over four hundred properties, including country houses, castles and gardens, which together attract more than ten million visits each year. (See Weideger 1994 for a critical analysis of the work of the National Trust.)

A complete exploration of all organisations or bodies responsible for the supply of rural tourism is, of course, beyond the scope of this chapter. However, within the context of the total rural tourism product concept, it is evident that both the public and private sectors play vital roles in the provision of rural tourism. These roles are not always distinct as there may be joint public–private sector provision and, furthermore, the position of the voluntary sector is not always clear. Nevertheless, for the purposes of this book, it is logical to consider the supply of rural tourism from the separate perspectives of the public and private sectors.

RURAL TOURISM: PUBLIC SECTOR SUPPLY

In a general sense it is the public sector that provides the broad framework within which specific opportunities for rural tourism are supplied. In other words, in most countries it is usually the state which, to a lesser or greater extent, defines and controls rural land use policies, which legislates for development or conservation in rural areas and which, through various forms of subsidy or support, directly and indirectly influences the supply of rural tourism. For example, as discussed in Chapter 2, agricultural and regional development policies throughout Europe have resulted in a significant increase in farm-related tourism initiatives.

At the same time, however, the state also plays a specific role in the provision of rural tourism, a role which, as Curry (1994: 49) suggests, is both necessary and justifiable for some or all of the following reasons:

- In many countries the public have always had the opportunity to gain access to rural areas for tourism and leisure purposes and the state has a duty to ensure that these opportunities are maintained.
- In some, but not all, areas, people have enjoyed a traditional or legal right of access to specific places or along specific routes and, again, it is the state's duty to safeguard these rights.
- In some instances it is only the public sector that is in the position to provide particular rural tourism facilities or opportunities, such as national parks or other designated land areas.
- It can be argued that rural tourism is a 'merit good'. In other words, the opportunity to participate in rural tourism can be considered to be good both for individuals and for society as a whole and should, therefore, be provided by the state.

The extent to which these four arguments represent valid grounds for public sector involvement in the supply of rural tourism is dependent on a number of factors and will vary from country to country. For example, the level and type of demand for rural tourism, the availability and suitability of rural areas for recreation, the existence of legal rights of access and even broader political factors may determine the state's role. However, given the increasingly diverse demands on rural areas, there is no doubt that some degree of public sector involvement is essential in order both to maintain opportunities for rural tourism and to control the commercial, private sector exploitation of the countryside as a resource for tourism and other uses. This involvement may be manifested in a number of ways and may be translated into the supply of specific attractions or facilities, such as state-run camp sites or country parks provided by local authorities. Here, however, we are concerned with more general issues and there are two ways, in particular, in which the state positively influences the supply of rural tourism. These are through the designation of land for rural tourism and through the provision or maintenance of access to the countryside.

Designating land for rural tourism

Land designation is a method by which the state attempts to intervene in or influence the use of a particular area of land. The actual purpose of designation may vary, although the prime objective is normally the protection or conservation of the landscape or flora and fauna, and there are also different means by which designation is imposed. In some cases, for example, the desired level of control may be achieved through the provision of financial incentives to landowners whereas, in other cases, taking land into public ownership may be seen as the most appropriate course of action.

Whatever the purpose and form of land designation, however, it generally signifies that particular areas of land are of national or international importance and, hence, worthy of protection.

There is an enormous variety of land designations. The International Union for the Conservation of Nature and Natural Resources (IUCN) has identified ten different categories of protected areas (Table 4.1), together covering more than 10,000 designated areas in Europe alone (FNNPE 1993), whilst each identified category also contains sub-categories; 'protected landscapes', for example, include the 27 Parcs Naturels Régionaux in France and the 41 Areas of Outstanding Natural Beauty in the UK.

However, within the context of this chapter, the most relevant category is national park designation, although many other designations, such as nature reserves or forest parks, are of course potential additions to the public sector supply of rural tourism.

National Parks

The importance of balancing the needs of tourists with the conservation and protection of the most popular yet fragile rural tourism destinations has long been recognised. The concept of national parks was first proposed by William Wordsworth who, in 1810, suggested that the English Lake District should be deemed a sort of 'national property', yet the world's first national park was designated in the United States at Yellowstone in 1872. It was almost eighty years later that legislation was passed to enable the designation of national parks in the UK (see MacEwan and MacEwan 1982, 1987; Blunden and Curry 1990) but, in the intervening period, many other countries established parks both to protect the rural environment and to provide opportunities for recreation. For example, Canada's first park, Rocky Mountain Park (later to be renamed Banff National Park) was established in 1887, whilst Europe's first national park was created in Sweden in 1909 (Hoggart *et al.* 1995).

However, at this early stage the designation of national parks was largely inspired by the potential for commercial gain resulting from the promotion of recreation rather than for altruistic reasons. Thus, Rocky Mountain Park was based upon the development of tourism at the Banff Hot Springs whilst even Yellowstone was established by the Yellowstone Park Act primarily as a 'pleasuring ground for the benefit and

Table 4.1 IUCN protected area categories

I	Scientific reserve/strict nature reserve
II	National park
III	Natural monument
IV	Managed nature reserve or wildlife sanctuary
V	Protected landscape
VI	Natural biotic area or anthropological reserve
VII	Multiple use management area/managed resource
IX	Biosphere reserve
X	World Heritage Site

Source: FNNPE (1993)

enjoyment of the people' (cited in McNamee 1993: 20). Indeed, it was not until 1916 that the National Parks Service in the United States was founded and two years later that the basic function of the US park system was established. For the first time, national parks were to be 'maintained in absolutely unimpaired form for the use of future generations as well as those of our time . . . [and] . . . set aside for the use, observation, health and pleasure of the people' (National Parks Service Annual Report 1918, cited in Albright and Cahn 1985: 69). As a result, one of the first tasks of the National Parks Service was to remove all existing tourism-related businesses that were deemed to be inappropriate or in excess of the requirements of the parks.

Nowadays, national parks are the most widespread and increasingly common form of public sector supplied rural tourism opportunities. In 1977, for example, the IUCN listed ninety countries with national parks or equivalent designations, with five of the top ten countries with the greatest area of parkland being in Africa (Wilkinson 1978); almost twenty years later, there are about 1500 national parks in 125 countries, accounting for 5 per cent of the world's land area (Mieczkowski 1995). Most national parks welcome tourists, but their prime purpose is not simply to provide for public enjoyment. It is no coincidence that some of the most popular rural tourism destinations are also the most beautiful and ecologically fragile and, therefore, national parks normally have the twin objectives of recreation provision and conservation. These aims are embodied in the IUCN's definition of national parks as areas which have not been 'materially altered by human exploitation and occupation . . . [and where] . . . visitors are allowed to enter, under special conditions, for inspirational, cultural and recreative purposes' (IUCN 1975). Furthermore, areas designated as national parks should be managed by the country's 'highest competent authority'. However, this definition is not universally applied as a basis for designating national parks and, as a result, the characteristics, numbers and roles of parks vary considerably from one country to another. For example, in England and Wales there are ten national parks, covering roughly 9 per cent of the land area (Figure 4.2), whereas the nineteen Polish national parks comprise just 0.8 per cent of Poland's land area (Baranowska-Janota 1994).

Similarly, Germany has just three parks compared with ten in Greece whilst, generally, most European national parks, unlike those in North America, 'have not emerged from a wilderness tradition but reflect a concern for the protection of environments that are strongly marked by human activities' (Hoggart *et al.* 1995: 244). For example, over a quarter of a million people live in the English and Welsh parks and such is their level of development that none appear in the IUCN's list of internationally recognised national parks. Conversely, in Scotland, arguably the most 'wilderness'-like area of the UK, there are no national parks at all. The following case study on national parks in Australia provides further evidence of the different approaches to park designation around the world.

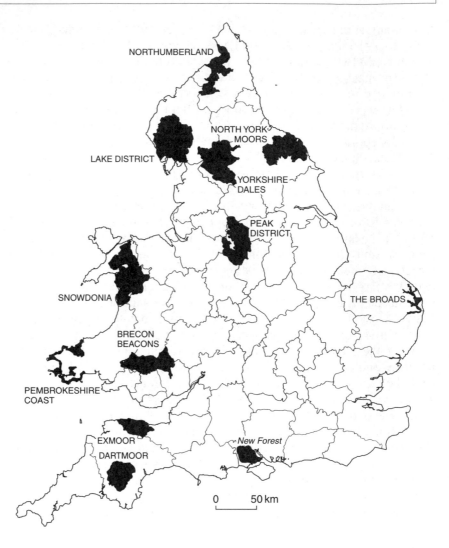

Figure 4.2 The national parks of England and Wales

Case study 6: The development of national parks in Australia

The first laws to protect scenic areas in Australia were passed in Tasmania as early as 1863 and just sixteen years later, in 1879, Australia's first national park was established near Sydney. Often described as the world's second national park (after Yellowstone in the United States), the designation of the Royal National Park represented the first step towards the development of a nationwide network of designated areas and, at the most recent count, there were about 3429 protected areas, conservation parks and refuges in Australia, together covering more than 50 million hectares, or 6.4 per cent of the total land area of the country. There are also 158 protected marine and estuarine areas, covering an additional 40 million hectares (Australia Tourist Commission 1995).

There is little doubt, therefore, that Australia has more national parks than any other country in the world; New South Wales alone boasts more than 70, roughly twice the number of national parks in the entire United States. However, rather than resulting from simply having a large number of sites worthy of protection, the enormous number of national parks and other designations in Australia is indicative of the historically different management and role attached to Australian national parks compared with those in other countries. For example, it is only since 1975, when the Australian National Parks and Wildlife Service was formed, that the Australian Federal Government has played an active part in park management and, even now, only five national parks, Kakadu, Uluru-Kata Tjuta (Ayers Rock and Mt Olga), Norfolk Island, Christmas Island and Jervis Bay, are under the direct federal management of the Australia Nature Conservation Agency. All other national parks are managed by state or territory bodies (Australia Tourist Commission 1995).

In a sense, therefore, most of Australia's national parks are not 'national' according to the IUCN definition (see above) and, certainly in the early days, the emphasis was on the provision of recreational opportunities rather than conservation. For example, the development of the Royal National Park, established in 1879 by the Colony of New South Wales, included holiday accommodation, tennis courts and picnic areas and most of the other national parks near Sydney are in existence today, not because the areas were deemed worthy of protection, but because the land was considered to be unsuitable for either agriculture or housing development (Pigram 1983). Similarly, in 1892, the Victorian government designated 600 hectares of Crown Land at Tower Hill as a national park for recreation, although not only did the government reserve the right to exploit the area for mining, road and railway development, reservoirs and so on, but the land had previously been cleared, grazed and quarried. As Boden and Baines (1981: 148) suggest, 'it was hardly an example of unspoiled Australian bushland'. Furthermore, in both of these cases, the management of the parks was the responsibility of a board of trustees who had virtually a free hand to develop the parks as they wished.

This pattern of national park designation was repeated across the country (see Black and Breckwoldt (1981) and even when Tasmania established its first national park at Mount Field in 1915, its primary purpose was for the pleasure and recreation of local people and tourists rather than conservation. Generally, then, the early national parks in Australia were relatively small areas of land which had previously been exploited (or were believed to have no development potential), they were set aside primarily for recreation, and they were managed independently both from each other and from state control.

Since these early days, the role of national parks in Australia has been broadened beyond the simple provision of recreation to include the conservation and environmental protection aims more generally considered to be one of the major purposes of national park designation. In 1970, the Fourth Ministerial Conference on National Parks agreed that a national park should be 'a relatively large area set aside for its features of predominantly unspoiled natural landscape, flora and fauna, permanently dedicated for public enjoyment, education and inspiration, and protected from all interference other than essential management practices, so that its natural attributes are preserved' (cited in Boden and Baines 1981). Although not binding on state governments, this has become a guiding objective in most states; there remains, nevertheless, a variety of definitions of national parks around Australia.

Another feature is that the management of Australia's national parks has become more centralised, at least at the state level. In New South Wales, the National Parks and Wildlife Act was passed in 1967, merging the previously separate responsibilities for park management and wildlife conservation, and similar legislation followed in Tasmania in 1970, in South Australia in 1972, in Queensland in 1975 and in the Northern Territory in 1976.

Nevertheless, the national park network in Australia has generally developed on an *ad hoc* basis, with the result that some areas of the country lack easily accessible recreation areas whereas others, perhaps, lack the protection they deserve. Furthermore, the Australian national parks face many of the problems and conflicts experienced in other parts of the world. For example, many of the more popular parks, such as the Blue Mountains National Park located just 120 kilometres from Sydney, face intense visitor pressures and impacts, yet entry charges to some parks contribute towards conservation work. At the same time, many Australian parks are prime international tourist attractions and with tourism contributing over A$11 billion to the economy in 1994, the economic importance of the national parks goes without saying. Thus, the conflicts between conservation and recreation provision are all too evident in many parks. Problems over land ownership within parks have also emerged in recent years; for example, Uluru (Ayers Rock) is one of the major tourist attractions of Australia, yet for thousands of years the rock was the focus of the religious and cultural activities of the Aboriginal peoples of the western desert and, to this day, the traditional owners of the area prefer tourists to respect their culture and not climb the rock.

Much of the controversy surrounding national parks in Australia results, it has been suggested (Boden and Baines 1981), from a lack of tolerance and compromise amongst relevant groups and individuals. This, in turn, may be seen as perhaps the inevitable result of the haphazard and localised approach to national park designation and the lack of a national policy throughout much of the history of the country's national park system. However, it is hoped that the management of the Kakadu National Park, located in the north of the country 250 kilometres east of Darwin, will provide a model for other parks in Australia to follow. Covering 19,804 square kilometres, Kakadu has three major rivers flowing through it and not only does it support a rich assortment of flora and fauna but it has also been home to Aborigines for at least 25,000 years. As a result, the area contains a wealth of cultural and historical sites. However, the park surrounds mining areas and therefore the management of the park involves the co-operation of both commercial interests and Aboriginal people, working in partnership with the Australian Nature Conservation Agency to determine park policy.

Despite these national differences in the character and meaning of national parks or equivalent designations, they all share the same purposes and, to a great extent, the same problems. In many, if not all, national parks, the relationship between conservation and tourism has become one of conflict (Budowski 1976) as tourism related developments and ever increasing numbers of tourists threaten to destroy their characteristics and qualities. This problem is particularly acute where tourism and national parks represent an important sector of the local or national economy (Marsh 1987) and it is now widely accepted that national parks have become victims of their own success; they are being 'loved to death' (FNNPE). In response, greater emphasis is now being placed on their conservation role (Edwards 1991) and on seeking ways of developing more sustainable or appropriate forms of tourism within national parks in particular and rural areas in general (Hill 1992; Countryside Commission 1995b).

There is an increasing body of literature concerned with tourism impacts and sustainable tourism planning and development (for example, see Inskeep 1991; Nelson *et al.* 1993; Coccossis and Nijkamp 1995). These issues within the context of rural tourism are considered in more detail in Chapter 6 but the important point here is that not only is national park designation the main way in which the public sector provides for rural tourism but also that national parks represent a model for tourism planning and management both in the wider countryside and more generally. In other words, nowhere is the relationship between tourism and the environment more evident, and potentially more conflicting, than in the world's national parks and they demonstrate, therefore, both the role and the broader responsibility of the public sector in the supply of rural tourism. (See also Pigram 1983 for an analysis of national parks.)

Access for rural tourism

Rural tourism, by definition, occurs in rural areas and, therefore, the great majority of tourists require sufficient and suitable means of access both to and within the countryside. At the same time, people's ability to participate in many rural tourism activities, such as hiking, climbing or camping, is entirely dependent on access to or through areas of the countryside where they may or may not enjoy an unrestricted or legal right of access. Moreover, as Millward (1993) argues, the increase in the demand for rural tourism during the latter half of the twentieth century, particularly in Western Europe, 'has not been matched by a similar increase in the supply of publicly accessible lands and routes *within* the countryside'. In fact, many traditional rights of access have been lost to encroaching urbanisation, forestry and modern farming methods (Shoard 1987). Thus, the issue of access is of fundamental importance to the supply of rural tourism and one which, perhaps inevitably, falls within the domain of the public sector as it is only the state which is in a position to influence the supply access, particularly in those countries where the rights of private landowners predominate.

The creation of national parks and other designated areas is one way in which the public sector provides access to rural areas. However, in these circumstances, even where the land is owned by the state, access is often restricted either by boundaries, entry charges or specific opening/closure times and is, therefore, controlled. Conversely, in the UK, with the exception of country parks which were designed specifically to increase the 'stock' of recreational facilities (Countryside Commission 1989a), the creation of national parks and other designated areas has not resulted in increased access as the great majority of the land concerned remains in private ownership.

Of greater relevance is the supply of publicly accessible land and routes in the wider, non-designated countryside and, for tourists, the potential 'freedom to roam'. Little, if any, comparative research has been undertaken into the availability of access in different countries (see Scott 1992) and the situation is further complicated by a variety of factors, such as geographical characteristics or rural tourism demand patterns, in different areas. Furthermore, there are different ways of conceptualising access. For example, Millward (1993) categorises access on a scale of 'increasing rigour', ranging from passive access (areas within 100 metres of roads passable by cars), through casual (along footpaths), vigorous and rugged access, to arduous access (in true wilderness). From this perspective, the more rugged an area, the less accessible it is to the 'average' tourist.

Generally, then, there is no universally applicable measure of access. Importantly, however, the supply of access can be determined by the extent to which tourists have a right of access, rather than by their ability to exercise those rights (see Countryside Commission 1986), and it is the state, through legislation and other means, which can determine the level of supply. At one extreme, public access to the countryside might be limited to areas set aside for recreation with all private land effectively 'off limits'; at the other extreme, visitors might be allowed to wander at will in the countryside. The latter situation is found in Sweden where, subject to certain conditions, visitors to the countryside enjoy *allemansrätt* (Colby 1988), or the legal right of access to all land, whether publicly or privately owned (see Figure 4.3).

A similar situation exists in Norway, where the great majority of the landscape is undeveloped and available for recreation. Visitors to the

Public access to Sweden's beautiful countryside is generally unrestricted and is governed by a centuries-old tradition known as 'Allemansrätt'. This means in principle that you can walk, ski or ride through any land, fields or wood without being turned back by the landowner. However, visitors to the countryside are requested to observe a few common-sense guidelines.

- Please show care and consideration towards other people, animals, plants and wildlife.
- You are generally allowed to walk across other people's land and sail on their water provided that you don't get too close to houses or walk over gardens or land under seed or crops.
- You can swim, moor your boat and go ashore, provided you do not go too close to houses or land in a prohibited area.
- Please do not camp close to houses, and ask the landowner for permission if you wish to pitch a group of tents or stay in one place for any length of time.
- Please do not light a fire if there is any risk of it spreading.
- You are not allowed to drive cars, caravans, motor homes, motor-bikes or mopeds off the road.
- Free fishing along Sweden's coasts and archipelagos is allowed only with rod and line.

Source: Adapted from Swedish Travel & Tourism Council (1995)

Figure 4.3 Public access in Sweden

Norwegian countryside enjoy the right of *Allemansretten*, the right of access to most private land, although subject to certain conditions laid down in legislation. Germany, too, has a right of public access (*Betretungsrecht*) enshrined in law, although this is restricted mainly to forests, unenclosed land and along roads and paths. In most countries, however, the degree of access falls between these two extremes and is determined by a number of factors, including:

- The existence of legal or traditional rights of access along particular routes or areas of land. Where no such rights exist, access is likely to be more limited than in countries such as England, where there is an extensive network of public rights of way.
- Patterns of land ownership and use. Studies have shown that where there are larger areas of intensively farmed land, with no history of communal access or land ownership, access will be more restricted (Millward 1992). Conversely, access is greater where there are smaller land holdings and a variety of land uses.
- The availability of open countryside relative to overall population density and the demand for rural tourism.
- Cultural or historical attitudes towards private land ownership and public access. In many parts of Scotland, for example, visitors are allowed the freedom to roam by custom, though not by legal right.
- The degree of countryside planning and related legislation and the willingness of the state to develop policies for public access in the countryside.

This list is by no means exhaustive and, as the popularity of newer forms of rural recreational activities increases, so too will the demand for greater access. The situation in the UK is of particular interest, where a relatively high population density, a high level of participation in rural tourism and very little accessibility to open, public land has placed the issue of access high on the rural tourism planning agenda. There, attention is focused on the 225,000 kilometre Public Rights of Way Network, a collection of footpaths, bridleways and byways that provide a legal right of access through the countryside, with significant efforts being made to maintain, repair and open up the entire network by the year 2000 (see Countryside Commission 1990b; Garner and Jones 1993; Sharpley 1996).

Thus, overall, the public sector plays a critical role in the supply of rural tourism and in balancing that supply with other demands on rural areas, including conservation. In many instances it also indirectly influences the supply of tourism through policies relating to social and economic development in the countryside, countryside planning, transport and so on, in effect setting the context within which the private sector operates.

RURAL TOURISM: PRIVATE SECTOR SUPPLY

The private sector comprises all the commercial organisations and businesses that, together, satisfy the various needs of rural tourists. Many supply the basic, traditional requirements of visitors, such as accommodation, food and drink or transport services and, given the emphasis placed on tourism as a means of diversifying and regenerating rural economies, it is not surprising that these businesses are increasing in number. However, many others are more directly involved in the supply of rural tourism inasmuch as they provide an enormous variety of attractions and activities, some of which complement the rural tourism experience whilst others represent the entire experience. For example, some forms of accommodation, such as farms, may be part of the desired 'rurality' of a visit to the countryside whilst inland resorts, such as the Center Parcs holiday villages in England and northern Europe, are located in rural areas but offer what is, in effect, a self-contained experience separate from the wider rural setting.

Such is the range and diversity of commercial organisations involved in the supply of rural tourism that even simply to list them all would be a difficult, if not impossible, task. However, the main point to consider here is the extent to which the private sector provision of facilities and opportunities conforms with, or contributes to, the development of the total rural tourism product, satisfying the demands and expectations of rural tourists whilst being appropriate to the broader development of rural areas. There are two sectors, in particular, which deserve attention: accommodation and attractions/activities.

Rural tourism: accommodation

Although rural tourism utilises virtually every type of accommodation, one of the most popular forms of tourism accommodation in the countryside is on farms. Indeed, in many countries, such as Germany and the UK, there is a long tradition of farm-based accommodation provision and, in some areas, it represents a significant proportion of the total accommodation stock; for example, around 18 per cent of tourist bed spaces in Austria are located on farms (Embacher 1994).

However, the emergence of a widespread supply of farm-based accommodation, particularly in Europe, is a relatively recent phenomenon (Hoyland 1982), resulting to a great extent from the need of rural economies to restructure and diversify. Thus, although farm accommodation is almost entirely supplied by the private sector, it is no coincidence that its development is frequently guided or encouraged by either national policies or specific organisations. A number of European countries, including France, Germany, Italy and Denmark, have specific national policies related to the promotion of farm tourism (Frater 1983), whilst Canada and the United States also have both national and state policies concerned with rural tourism in general and farm tourism in particular (Butler and Clark 1992).

Perhaps the best example of this has been the development of 'gîte' accommodation in France. In the mid 1950s, the French Ministry of Agriculture initiated the 'gîtes rureaux prives' scheme by offering financial support to farmers who wished to redevelop old or redundant buildings into accommodation. Since then, the gîte concept has expanded to include accommodation facilities not only on farms but also in rural cottages, converted mills and even in châteaux accommodation. The supply of gîtes is also supported by marketing organisations, such as Gîtes de France, which offer complete holiday packages, including transport, in gîte accommodation. All such accommodation is privately owned, offers self-catering only, is rural in character and bears the trademark of quality of the 'Fédération Nationale des Gîtes Ruraux de France', guaranteeing the standard of accommodation. The gîte movement has, therefore, been instrumental in supplementing farm incomes and maintaining the character and structure of rural France (Frater 1983) whilst offering a variety of reasonably priced rural accommodation.

Farm-based accommodation also includes the provision of bed and breakfast and camping and caravanning facilities and surveys have shown that tourists are attracted to all forms of farm accommodation by the rural setting, the peace and quiet and value for money (see, for example, Denman and Denman 1993). However, one of the major challenges facing the farm accommodation sector is marketing and promotion (see Chapter 5), and it is also interesting to note that some commentators have suggested that, despite the emphasis placed on the supply of accommodation facilities as a means of diversifying and maintaining farm incomes, a number of factors, such as low profit margins and potential oversupply, mean that reliance on farm tourism as a 'worthy activity capable of resolving the social and economic problems in rural areas is . . . fundamentally misguided' (Maude and van Rest 1985; see also Crocker 1986).

There is, of course, an enormous variety of other forms of rural tourism accommodation. Bed and breakfast in private houses, the private letting of second homes, camping and caravanning, youth hostels and bunk barns (basic overnight accommodation for hikers) may all be included although a precise definition and quantification is impossible owing to the informal nature of much of the supply and the problems of defining rural tourism. However, rural hotels are an important addition to the overall supply of accommodation. In Europe, these tend to be smaller, independent, family-run establishments, although in France the 'Logis de France' and 'Auberges de France' are national, voluntary chains of one- and two-star hotels whose members conform to certain standards and rural characteristics (Grolleau 1987). More prestige establishments are also to be found in most countries and are frequently based upon country mansions, stately homes or castles; the Spanish Paradores (see Case study 7) or Country House hotels in the UK fall into this category. Finally, it is also important to point out that not all rural accommodation is necessarily supplied by the private sector. For example, camp sites may be run by the state, in the UK the Forestry Commission provides holiday cabins for rent and, as discussed in the following case study, the network of Spanish Paradores is state-owned.

Case study 7: The Paradores of Spain

Owing to the popularity of Spain as a sun-sea-sand holiday destination, the great majority of tourist accommodation in the country is to be found in the highly developed tourism regions along the Mediterranean coastline. For example, the Balearic Islands account for almost a quarter of all registered bed spaces in Spain whilst Catalonia, which includes the popular Costa Brava, supplies a further 20 per cent of bed spaces (see Valenzuela 1991; Albert-Piñole 1993). Most of this accommodation is of the modern hotel/apartment variety, although camping is also popular; Catalonia alone provides over 40 per cent of all campsite spaces in the country.

However, tourism in Spain is not, of course, restricted to the coastal areas and a variety of tourism accommodation is to be found throughout the country. This ranges from luxury hotels to the more basic pensions, or boarding houses, but one of the more notable forms of accommodation, particularly within the context of rural tourism, is the national network of Paradores.

The word *parador* literally means inn or stopping place and it was traditionally used to describe overnight lodgings offered to more respected or better-off travellers; more basic accommodation including stables for animals was provided by the *posada*. In 1926, the then Royal Tourist Commissioner suggested that this traditional concept of the parador could be developed into a nationwide network of accommodation facilities, the basic philosophy being that the state should be responsible for the supply of hotel accommodation in those areas where it would be neither realistic nor profitable for the private sector to do so. Furthermore, it was intended that, by utilising old castles, monasteries and palaces, the development of Paradores would play a significant role in the preservation of historically and culturally important buildings and monuments whilst at the same time creating employment in some of the less developed regions of the country.

The first Parador was established in the Gredos mountain range with the specific purpose of providing accommodation for visitors participating in hunting and, since then, the chain of state-owned Paradores has expanded to a total of 86 establishments, 83 of which are hotels and the remaining three are *Hosterias*, or restaurants. The distribution of Paradores is shown in Figure 4.4.

Of the 35 based upon renovated historic buildings, 13 are medieval castles, 8 are convents and hospitals, 7 are baroque or gothic palaces, 5 are old manor houses and 2 have been built in historic surroundings. The rest are modern constructions, albeit built in a style that is sympathetic to the environment. Together, the Paradores provide 8500 beds in 4500 rooms and in 1990 they attracted a total of more than 1.7 million

Figure 4.4 The distribution of Paradores in Spain

overnight stays. Thus, although they attract a more specialist and up-market clientele, Paradores represent a unique form of tourist accommodation in rural areas whilst fulfilling many of the objectives of tourism as a means of rural development and diversification. Moreover, they have played an important role in the state's attempts to encourage the development of inland tourism to spread the benefits of tourism away from the popular coastal areas

Source: Juez (1991)

Overall, then, the supply of rural tourism accommodation satisfies a range of tourist requirements whilst, by and large, contributing to local development needs. Some forms of accommodation are, however, controversial. Modern, purpose-built holiday villages or club-share complexes in rural settings are often criticised as being inappropriate within the rural context and of relatively little economic benefit to local communities, whilst second- or holiday-home ownership has a major impact on the availability and price of houses for local residents.

Rural tourism: attractions and activities

The major attraction of rural tourism has traditionally been, and for many still remains, the countryside itself. During the early development of rural tourism, most visitors were satisfied with opportunities for enjoying the physical and cultural characteristics of the countryside and there was relatively little need for additional attractions. However, these early attitudes and expectations of rural tourists have been replaced in more recent years by demands for higher quality and higher standards of service and comfort and 'above all, a supply of activities to keep the holidaymakers entertained and active during their stay' (Davidson 1992: 143). In other words, it has been increasingly recognised that, in order to attract visitors to the countryside in the first place and to keep them there once they have arrived, it is necessary to supply a variety of attractions both to entertain them and, from a pragmatic point of view, to give them more opportunities to contribute towards the local rural economy.

The private sector plays a dominant role in providing a vast range of attractions and activities in the countryside or by facilitating people's participation in particular activities. For example, the popularity of hiking and its development into a year-round, all-weather activity has been aided greatly by the production and widespread supply of modern equipment and clothing. Many attractions and activities have evolved as a result of the development of farm tourism; farm visitor centres, farm museums, self-guided farm trails, farm shops, educational visits, demonstrations, nature studies or pick-your-own sites are all farm-based attractions, whilst a number of different activities, including horse-riding, fishing and shooting, are widely available on farms (Clarke 1996).

A large number of other attractions and activities are also supplied by the private sector. Many attractions are directly related to the rural environment, such as vineyards, wild animal sanctuaries, private nature reserves and woodlands, birds of prey centres, and so on, whilst facilities and opportunities for virtually any activity that occurs in or depends upon the countryside, from land or water based activities to aerial activities, such as hang-gliding or hot-air ballooning, are available. For example, eighteen different companies operate river activities on the Colorado in the Grand Canyon National Park in the United States and at least three offer flights through the canyon (Zube and Galante 1994). Complete rural holidays are also supplied by the private sector, ranging from educational or health visits to hiking, canal cruising, cycling holidays and even wine-tasting tours, whilst conservation holidays, where people work on conservation projects in rural areas, have become increasingly popular both in developed and developing countries. In short, the countryside is widely exploited as a tourism resource by the private sector.

Increasingly, however, what may be described as rural heritage is also being packaged and sold as a tourist attraction. That is, a heritage 'industry' (Hewison 1987, 1989) has been developed around the real or imagined society and culture of rural life, past and present. The opening of historic houses, castles, gardens and rural industrial centres are part of this industry, as are craft shows or demonstrations and countryside festivals, but attractions and destinations are also being developed around what may be described as an imagined rural heritage. In other words, past events or characteristics of rural culture are interpreted and supplied to tourists in a variety of ways, from rural heritage centres to staged reconstructions of events, presenting an idealised or 'rose-tinted' version of the past. For example, it has been suggested that images of the 'Old West' in the United States have been reasserted by the promotion of 'Indian cultures, archaeological sites, and dude ranches' in states such as Colorado and Utah (Zube and Galante 1994: 230) whilst, in the UK, the presentation of rural heritage is based upon an image of a pre-industrial, unspoiled and, frequently, literary landscape (see Olwig 1989; Phillips 1989; Wright 1985).

The use of heritage as a tourist attraction is the subject of much wider debate. The important point here, however, is that the countryside provides an enormous variety of commercial opportunities for the private sector of the tourism industry which, in turn, supplies an increasingly diverse range of activities and attractions. Many of these may be considered to be appropriate to the rural setting but others, such as theme parks, golf courses or motorised sports activities, may be seen as out of place in the countryside.

CONCLUSION

The supply of rural tourism is a complex process. The rural tourism product comprises more than simply the attractions, facilities and recreational opportunities that are offered in a rural setting. To many visitors, the general rural environment or the concept of 'rurality', either actual or perceived, is as much a part the rural tourism experience as are, for example, accommodation facilities. Furthermore, rural tourism occurs within a multi-purpose, fragile resource, the countryside, which is normally under private ownership. Therefore, rural tourism is supplied not only by the myriad of smaller, private sector businesses which, typically, make up the rural tourism industry, but also by a variety of public sector agencies. The latter may include organisations with specific responsibilities for the provision of recreational opportunities, such as national park authorities or tourist boards, or those with responsibilities indirectly linked to tourism, such as rural development agencies.

Together, the public and private sectors need to satisfy both the specific and broader needs and expectations of visitors to ensure that tourism, as one use of the rural resource, continues to contribute to the economic and social well-being of the countryside and its communities. However, at the same time, it is essential that the supply of rural tourism is balanced with the other uses of the countryside and, therefore, by implication, effective communication and co-operation is required between all those organisations involved. One way of achieving this is through the appropriate and co-ordinated marketing of rural tourism, and this forms the subject of the next chapter.

QUESTIONS

1. Explain the primary role of the public sector in the supply of rural tourism.
2. How applicable is the concept of the total tourism product to the examination of the supply of rural tourism?
3. What are the major problems and conflicts commonly occurring in national parks, and how might these be overcome?
4. Why is the provision of access one of the most important issues in the supply of rural tourism?

FURTHER READING

FNNPE (1993) *Loving them to Death? Sustainable Tourism in Europe's Nature and National Parks*, Grafenau: Federation of Nature and National Parks of Europe.
MacEwan, A. and MacEwan, M. (1982) *National Parks: Conservation or Cosmetics?*, London: George Allen & Unwin.
Pigram, J. (1983) *Outdoor Recreation and Resource Management,* London: Croom Helm.
Watkins, C. (ed.) (1996) *Rights of Way: Policy, Culture and Management*, London: Pinter.

Marketing the countryside for tourism $\boxed{5}$

INTRODUCTION

It has been suggested that the effective marketing of rural tourism is an attempt to achieve the impossible (Bonnetaud 1993). Certainly, when one considers that rural tourism is the aggregate of thousands of rural products (goods and services) offered to countless groups of customers by a combination of private and public sector organisations, it is not surprising that the marketing of rural tourism is seen as an impossible task.

However, this dispersion and fragmentation of the rural tourism product, whilst complicating the task of marketing rural tourism, also underlines the need *for* it. In other words, it is because there is no systematic or coherent organisation of the physical and human components of the products in rural tourism (Bonnetaud 1993) that the techniques of marketing and management are needed in order to help match the diverse elements of rural tourism to the needs and wants of potential purchasers. As Middleton (1995: 337) suggests in relation to marketing tourism in general, 'without management decisions there is no automatic . . . harmony between the multiple components of the overall tourism product, which are seldom under the same ownership'.

To make any sense of marketing rural tourism, it is important to consider the rural tourism product and its marketing from a number of different perspectives. These will largely depend upon the organisations involved, how they define the business they are in and, therefore, whom they consider their customers to be. For example, the approach of a regional tourist office towards marketing in a rural area will be significantly different from that of the proprietor of a tea shop.

In the 1970s, Medlik and Middleton (1973) identified the two main approaches taken by organisations in relation to the marketing of tourism products which have formed the basis for much of the subsequent work on this subject. First, marketing is concerned with the *overall* tourism product, which consists of all the elements consumed by the tourist from the time he or she leaves home until the time of return (see Chapter 4 for a discussion of the components of the 'total rural tourism product'). In the context of both rural and non-rural tourism, this is the usual perspective adopted by local, regional and national tourism offices and commercial tourism organisers who assemble a number of tourism elements and sell them as one. Secondly, marketing takes place in relation to the specific, often commercially-oriented products which together comprise the over-all tourism product, such as transport, attractions, accommodation and other facilities.

These two approaches, that is, either the overall marketing of rural places or destinations or the marketing of specific rural tourism products, form the basis of this chapter. However, although this dual-perspective provides a useful starting point, in reality the picture is much more complicated and, therefore, the main aim of the chapter is to highlight the major obstacles which prevent the effective marketing of rural tourism at all levels and to consider suggested ways of overcoming them. In particular, it outlines the concept and application of marketing in relation to the different organisations involved in rural tourism and emphasises the need for a more widespread and co-ordinated adoption of marketing techniques amongst them. First, however, it is important to define briefly what is meant by marketing.

WHAT IS MARKETING?

Marketing is neither an exact science, nor an art (Jefferson and Lickorish 1988). It is, perhaps, best described as a 'body of underlying concepts which form a guide to organisational and managerial thinking, planning and action' (Cooper *et al.* 1993: 223) and, whilst an in-depth analysis of the fundamentals of marketing is beyond the scope of this chapter, it is nevertheless essential to consider the basic definition and concept of marketing and its relevance to the rural tourism industry.

Many attempts have been made to define marketing. However, two of the most widely quoted are those of the Chartered Institute of Marketing (CIM) in the UK, which defines marketing as 'the management process responsible for identifying, anticipating and satisfying customers' requirements profitably', and Philip Kotler, who defines marketing as the 'social and managerial process by which individuals and groups obtain what they want and need through creating, offering and exchanging products of value with others' (Kotler 1991). Although Kotler's definition is, arguably, more appropriate to non-profit organisations, implicit in both are two propositions:

● Marketing is a philosophy of business or management orientation, whereby all the activities of an organisation are centred around meeting the needs of its customers or, more simply, based on customer orientation.
● Marketing is a management process which puts that philosophy of customer orientation into practice.

Marketing as a philosophy of business

The logic of seeing marketing first and foremost as a philosophy of business, whereby the focus of the whole organisation is the customer, is easy to grasp when it is considered that, in simple terms, businesses cannot exist without customers. In other words, for any business to survive, it not only needs to attract customers in the first place, but it must continually ensure that it is keeping its customers by satisfying their requirements.

Rural tourism, like any other business activity, needs to embrace this philosophy. Not only does it compete with other forms of tourism and leisure pursuits for a share of household disposable income, but it also competes with a whole range of other essential and non-essential household purchases, such as cars or 'white goods'. Therefore, it is important that the rural tourism industry is aware of the need to focus its activities around the needs of potential tourists or, in other words, to market its products effectively.

However, tourism is lagging behind other industries in the application of good marketing practice and, historically, the matching of needs, wants and perceived value to tourism products has been based upon 'intuitive judgement or hunch' (Jefferson and Lickorish 1988) rather than on a planned, logical process. Clearly, although intuition and creativity in marketing are both desirable and necessary, in today's dynamic and diverse economic and social environment it is not enough to rely on educated guesswork to determine customer requirements. It would be a mistake, for example, for individual tourism organisations to assume that, where the rural environment is one of the main attractions to tourists, no further marketing effort is required on their part to attract and keep custom. Hence, the need to be customer-oriented must be backed up by a systematic process of implementation, this process being the second aspect of 'what marketing is'.

Marketing as a management process

It is often mistakenly believed that the marketing process is something which is carried out only by the marketing departments of large organisations. In reality, however, it is a process which should penetrate all aspects of every business, no matter how large or small. In other words, marketing is an organisation-wide process. Therefore, the major challenge facing the marketer is to ensure that *all* the activities and functions of an organisation are geared towards the goal of customer satisfaction, a task that is as relevant to a hill farmer developing small-scale rural tourism as it is to the marketing director of a large, international airline.

The marketing management process broadly necessitates identifying what the customer needs and wants, followed by meeting those needs and wants within the limitations of the organisation's resources and the competitive and external environments. Figure 5.1 illustrates the consumer (or customer segments) as the core focus of the organisation, around which all management decisions are made.

Cooper *et al.* (1991: 236) have usefully compartmentalised these management decisions into a series of tasks (see Table 5.1), all of which form part of the marketing process which begins and ends with the customer (Figure 5.2).

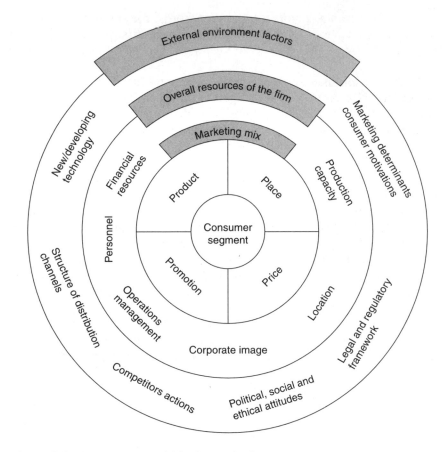

Figure 5.1 The consumer within the marketing system
Source: Adapted from Middleton (1988)

Table 5.1 Management tasks within the marketing process

Task	Marketing function
Identifying the customers needs	Marketing research
Analysing marketing opportunities	Analysis and selection of target markets
Translating needs into products	Product planning and formulation
Determining the product's value to the customer at different seasonal periods	Pricing policy
Making the product available	Distribution
Informing and motivating the customer	Promotion

These tasks are, broadly, marketing research, market analysis and segmentation, product planning and development, pricing, and the use of

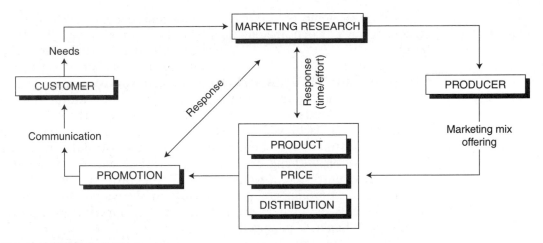

Figure 5.2 The marketing process
Source: Cooper *et al.* (1993: 236)

distribution channels and promotion. A large body of literature can be found on the implementation of these marketing techniques or tasks in general (for example, see Kotler 1991; Baker 1991; Cowell 1984) and on tourism marketing in particular (for example, Holloway and Plant 1992; Middleton 1988).

APPLYING THE MARKETING CONCEPT TO RURAL TOURISM

It has already been established that, from a supply point of view, rural tourism is characterised by a large number of private enterprises, many of which are profit-driven and which are able to narrowly define the business they are in. Given this, it is easy to see that the definition and concept of marketing outlined above fits well with the idea, for example, of running an activity centre or tea shop in the countryside.

However, it is a commonly held belief that a marketing approach is not necessarily appropriate, or even possible, for many organisations involved directly and indirectly with tourism in the countryside. First, not all activities within rural tourism are organised by profit-motivated businesses. The wider picture of planning, conservation and access and, in some cases, tourism promotion in rural areas belongs to an array of local and national public sector and quasi non-governmental organisations ('quango's'), as well as trusts, charities, chambers of commerce and voluntary bodies. All of these organisations 'market' aspects of the countryside to the general public (their customers) in some way or another, but none necessarily has financial profit as the over-riding objective. For example, countryside conservation, education, the benefits to health of outdoor recreation or appeals for financial support are all non-profit messages that may be communicated to potential countryside visitors. Even national or regional tourist boards and marketing consortia which operate commercially tend to have an indirect profit motive; that is, their main objectives are, usually, to increase visitor numbers, their length of stay and spending, and to counter seasonality in a region, thereby increasing the profits of their *members'* businesses.

The second major difficulty in applying the concept of marketing here is linked to the traditional marketing concept of customer orientation or, in other words, formulating and presenting the product to provide for the demands of the customer. In rural areas, there is always a balance to be achieved between 'the eternal triangle of visitor segments, destination resources, and residents' (Middleton 1996). Therefore, when utilising or exploiting a fragile and finite resource such as the countryside, it would be highly inappropriate, from both a social and an environmental point of view, to always provide what the customer wants, no matter how attractive it may appear from a purely commercial, business perspective.

Given these perceived difficulties of including non-profit organisations and wider social and environmental concerns in the traditional framework of marketing, it is hardly surprising that there has been an initial negative reaction of managers in the countryside towards marketing and that they 'consider commercialisation, brash advertising and profit motives as [marketing's] overriding goals' (Gilbert 1989). However, as rational as this reaction may seem, it is argued that the presumed difficulties of applying marketing techniques to rural tourism are generally based upon a misunderstanding of what marketing is all about. In reality, 'the principles of the body of knowledge about marketing and its main theoretical elements can be applied in all industries and in commercial and non-profit sectors of the economy' (Middleton 1988: 31). It is simply in the *application* of these principles that differences occur.

The marketing concept: non-profit organisations

Non-profit organisations, by definition, do not normally have financial gain as a principal objective although, in many countries, increasing numbers of public sector organisations have either been privatised or are being expected to develop their commercial activities in order to become more self-supporting. For example, the soon to be privatised Agricultural and Development Advice Service (ADAS) in the UK now offers fee-based consultancy, as opposed to free advice, to customers. Nevertheless, referring back to Kotler's definition of marketing given earlier, non-profit organisations still provide a *service of value* to *customers*, very often *in exchange* for taxes levied. Moreover, it is necessary for these organisations to satisfy their clients as they will not wish to be subject to widespread criticism and there may be substitutes to which the public can resort if the offering is poor (Kotler 1975). A marketing orientation, therefore, is just as applicable to non-profit motivated organisations as it is to commercial businesses and, whilst they may not need to satisfy customers' requirements '*profitably*', they will certainly be expected to do so '*efficiently*'.

The marketing concept: social and environmental concerns

Similarly, whilst it may appear that social and environmental concerns do not form part of a marketing orientation, these concerns should, arguably, be implicit in an organisation's marketing approach. That is, in considering how it can best meet the needs of its customers, an organisation will have to bear in mind the limitations of its own resources and those of the competitive and external environments (see Figure 5.1); these will, inevitably, include social and environmental factors. For example, externally imposed limitations will include the legal and planning framework dictated by central and local government, and may also include codes of conduct or accepted social and environmental practice imposed by industry societies and membership organisations. Internally, a rural tourism enterprise will also need to safeguard those environmental and social aspects of its product over which it has some control and which will affect product quality and, hence, the enterprise's ability to stay in business.

All of these considerations will affect the extent to which an organisation can or cannot develop its product offering to meet customer needs. In some circumstances, environmental and social limitations may be so great that the rural product cannot be adapted at all. However, this still does not prevent a marketing orientation; in these circumstances, the focus of marketing is to find those potential customers whose needs would be met by the product as it exists and to market it to them. In other words, marketing can also be about moulding demand around a fixed supply.

Thus, social and environmental concerns should evidently form part of a marketing orientation. However, governments are not usually able to legislate to cover, or enforce, all the potential problems of tourism development in the countryside and, in practice, organisations are only likely to take account of social or environmental factors in their marketing if they are legally bound to do so or if overlooking them would negatively impact on the success of their business. Therefore, as marketing activities within the rural tourism industry may frequently affect local communities or have implications beyond an organisation's immediate business environment, it is useful to look briefly at two variations of the basic concept of marketing which have been developed in recognition of the need for the adoption of broader social and environmental principles in marketing.

Social marketing, green marketing and sustainability

Social marketing evolved in the late 1960s and early 1970s as part of the growing concern for the environment, for consumer rights and for the disadvantaged within society. It was thought that marketing campaigns should be assessed for their impact on society as a whole and for the potential impacts which might arise not only between one group of consumers and another, but also between certain consumers and the needs of society. Social marketing is also concerned with emphasising the value and benefits of a resource or product to society and, therefore, this area of marketing is mainly associated with public sector and voluntary organisations which, in theory, have sufficient resources to mount influential social campaigns and to promote those things, such as outdoor recreation, that are thought to be 'good for us'.

However, social marketing is limited in its application to rural tourism because, although it features a high degree of societal concern, it does not set exacting environmental standards. Green marketing, on the other hand, is a more recent approach which encompasses the principles of social marketing but which differs from it, according to Peattie (1992), in the following ways:

- it has an open-ended rather than a long-term perspective;
- it focuses more strongly on the natural environment;
- it treats the environment as something that has an intrinsic value over and above its usefulness to society;
- it focuses on global concerns rather than on those of particular societies.

Together, social marketing and green marketing are designed to foster a more sustainable marketing approach (see Chapter 6) and their principles have already been adopted by a number of public sector organisations, not only in their own marketing but also in the guidelines for marketing which they, in turn, produce. For example, the English Tourist Board's guide to sustainable tourism (ETB 1991) suggests the following to tourism businesses:

- be honest and substantiate your environmental claims;
- identify your product's environmental benefits;
- undertake product-market matching;
- present details of the environment surrounding your operation;
- use recycled paper for all printed materials;
- consider developing environmental promotions .

However, the ideas of social and green marketing are just as important for commercial organisations in rural tourism and they are also gradually accepting the wisdom of a more sustainable approach. Middleton and Hawkins (1993) have argued that commercial tourism organisations have a vested interest in adopting a more socially and environmentally responsible approach to all their activities and that marketing has a central role in this. That is, consumers are becoming increasingly particular about the condition of the social and physical environment in which they spend their leisure time and organisations should react to this through their marketing process. In addition, the synergistic nature of rural tourism implies that each rural tourism business should have some degree of concern for the interests and survival of the next. As Middleton (1996) points out, 'sustainability or degradation through tourism at particular localities emerges *collectively* from the individual marketing processes of businesses'. It is, therefore, important to ensure that every organisation in rural tourism considers its own responsibility in the marketing of rural areas. The following section looks, in particular, at the roles and responsibilities of public sector organisations.

RURAL TOURISM MARKETING: PUBLIC SECTOR ROLES

The role of the public sector in the marketing of rural tourism is normally associated with broad, overarching promotional campaigns and messages to encourage visitors to a certain area or region. However, whilst this has traditionally been one important area of involvement for public sector organisations, their roles are, in fact, many, varied, often conflicting, and take place on a local, regional and national scale. These can be considered under three broad headings as discussed in the following sections.

Marketing and social access to the countryside

The countryside has long been appreciated for its role as the green lungs of the world's towns and cities. It is often perceived as a free resource from which everyone should be able to benefit and, in most countries in the industrialised world, there are government departments or agencies which endeavour to encourage the population to enjoy active pursuits for health reasons. In England, for example, this role is undertaken at the national level by both the Countryside Commission and the Sports Council.

Public sector promotion has traditionally been the means of achieving this objective but, as rural tourism is an activity participated in by a relatively narrow section of the population, it has been recognised that a more directed and strategic approach is required. In other words, to encourage people to visit the countryside who, for whatever reason, have not normally done so, it is important to identify different market segments, such as ethnic minority groups or the elderly, and to devise marketing plans that more closely reflect their specific needs.

In particular, market research is beginning to play an important role in discovering the physical and psychological barriers to participation amongst certain groups in society and what, if necessary, can be done to overcome them. For example, in the state of Ohio in the United States, research into the constraints to urban park usage amongst individuals with low incomes found that fear of crime, lack of companionship and transport problems were some of the factors which prevented wider usage. Similar research is needed in relation to the use of the broader countryside for tourism and recreation and, in particular, to the needs of customers who are increasingly older, urban, and racially and ethnically diverse (Dwyer 1994).

The problem with this sort of approach to the 'social marketing' of the countryside is that, as discussed earlier, there are obvious difficulties in changing aspects of the countryside resource to fit the particular needs of certain user groups. Indeed, many conservationists would argue that the countryside should only be enjoyed in its 'natural', challenging state and that the provision of extra facilities, such as hard-surfaced paths for wheelchairs and pushchairs, specially-installed gates or the waymarking of trails, degrades and sanitises the natural environment and leads to its over-use. Moreover, there is a growing school of thought which suggests that the image of the countryside as a 'free' good should be altered and that access for recreation should be restricted to those who are able or willing to pay for it (see Chapter 7). Thus, it could be argued that marketing the countryside for social tourism and recreation directly conflicts with another public sector marketing goal: conservation.

Marketing and countryside conservation and education

Conservation is not an aim that is commonly associated with marketing. However, marketing – and a marketing approach – is playing an increasingly important role in the public sector's efforts to protect the rural environment, particularly in relation to demand management and visitor education within the context of sustainable rural tourism development.

One of the major conservation challenges facing public sector organisations is the need to control the level of demand at specific rural tourism and recreation sites where over-use causes sometimes irreversible damage. Careful market research into the ways in which certain groups and individuals use these sites can help organisations to get the right conservation messages to the right people and to match the right sort of demand with the right sort of countryside. Moreover, where a rural attraction appeals to a large cross-section of different user groups, market research and product planning can contribute to the formulation of measures to meet different needs in the most sustainable way. For example, at many popular countryside sites it has been found that a large proportion of visitors are not necessarily interested in viewing a natural attraction at first hand; in fact, their needs can be met by providing a representation of the site with information and interpretation at a visitor centre. Thus, in meeting the needs of groups of customers such as these more closely, the experience of the whole site may be improved as only those who are strongly motivated to view the natural attraction will do so. This will be especially true if there is an 'effort-price' to pay, such as a reasonable walk or a bus-ride from the visitor centre.

However, the techniques of visitor management, interpretation and education, and the use of market research in their application, are not new and there is an extensive body of literature concerning both the interpretation of natural or heritage sites (see, for example, Uzzell 1989) and the zoning of rural areas for different uses (Murphy 1985; Gunn 1994). Nevertheless, it has been argued that, until recently, 'interpreters have been using market research rather as a drunk uses a lamp post – for support *not* illumination' (Stevens 1989: 104). In other words, rather than using market research as a guide to innovative ways of appealing to different identifiable user groups, it has simply been used to justify existing approaches which appeal to the lowest common denominator. Stevens (1989: 104) goes on to say that 'our challenge today is to ensure that interpretation is

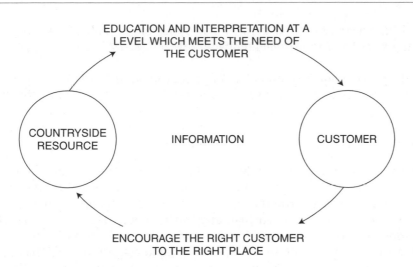

EDUCATION AND INTERPRETATION AT A
LEVEL WHICH MEETS THE NEED OF
THE CUSTOMER

COUNTRYSIDE
RESOURCE

INFORMATION

CUSTOMER

ENCOURAGE THE RIGHT CUSTOMER
TO THE RIGHT PLACE

Figure 5.3 The marketing–conservation relationship

based upon our understanding of the resource being interpreted, and understanding the character and nature of our customers.' Quite evidently, there is no point in attempting either to provide effective educational information for conservation purposes or to attempt to influence visitor behaviour without knowing your audience.

Figure 5.3 summarises the relationship between marketing and countryside conservation.

Another, more extreme, approach sometimes adopted by public sector and other organisations for conservation purposes is to 'de-market' an area. This technique is designed to decrease demand without the need for actual physical constraints by either simply not marketing the area or attraction in question or by appealing to potential visitors to avoid it. One example of a rural destination that has been subject to de-marketing is the Lyke Wake Walk, a popular circular route in North Yorkshire, England, that became so eroded through over-use that the local authorities had the trail removed from all Ordnance Survey maps. However, they could not prevent the continued sale of guide books which promote the walk, indicating that the effect of de-marketing is limited when several sources of information about a resource or attraction exist.

Marketing and economic development

The rationale for the economic development and regeneration of rural areas has already been discussed in previous chapters, with the public sector playing a lead role in the encouragement of rural economic growth through tourism. It has also been emphasised that the techniques of marketing cannot be separated from this development process if rural tourism products are to be created and promoted to satisfy potential demand.

Traditionally, the rural tourism marketing role in public sector organisations has been approached on two levels:

- through overall area umbrella image or promotional campaigns beneath which individual private sector organisations are expected to develop;
- through marketing facilitation, by providing help in the form of grants, training, consultancy or distribution advice to individual organisations to improve their own marketing efforts.

The most visible of these public sector roles in rural tourism marketing is, of course, image projection. Above and beyond the use of rural images for regional tourism promotional purposes, the countryside image is, perhaps, more widely utilised than any other to sell tourism destinations worldwide. For example, the image of rice-pickers in front of the Karst limestone towers in Guilin is frequently used to sell southern China in the same way that a typical village featuring stone cottages would be an inevitable part of an international promotion of Britain or that the dramatic rock formations of Monument Valley, seen in countless 'westerns', usually feature in promotional material for the United States. In every case, market analysis and assessment of different broad target audiences will help to define the image which should be conveyed, with different 'versions' of the countryside being promoted to different national, regional or other defined groups.

However, tourism promotion organisations must be careful not to misrepresent the rural tourism product by carefully selecting words and pictures which present a 'romantic gaze' (Urry 1990a: 46) bearing little relation to reality. In much promotion of the British countryside, for example, 'nowhere is there the increasingly common sprawl of ribbon development, the clutter of signs, electricity pylons and telegraph wires, the bungalows on the hill tops, the roundabouts and the bypasses round the villages. Any sign of urbanisation of the countryside simply is carefully edited out' (Clark *et al.* 1994: 162).

Similarly, in recent years regional tourist organisations have found that successful movies, television shows or books which reinforce this positive, romantic view of the countryside have generated interest in the rural areas featured. For example, following the success of the film *Braveheart* at the 1996 Academy Awards, the Scottish Tourist Board was anticipating a significant increase in the number of visitors, worth an extra £16 million in tourism revenue, in much the same way as the number of American tourists visiting Australia increased by 25 per cent in the years following the release of the film *Crocodile Dundee*. Case study 8 describes the way in which literary associations may also be used to market a rural area as a tourism destination.

Case study 8: Brontë Country Tourism

In 1820, the Reverend Patrick Brontë moved with his wife and six children to the small village of Haworth in Yorkshire, England. The family lived in the Georgian parsonage in the village and it was there that three of the Brontë sisters, Charlotte, Emily and Anne, wrote their famous novels, including *Jane Eyre*, *Wuthering Heights* and *The Tenant of Wildfell Hall*, during the 1840s. Since then, as a result of the Brontë sisters' books and the moorland scenery which inspired their work, a thriving tourism industry has been built up in the area. The Brontë family home, now the Brontë Parsonage Museum, alone attracts over 100,000 visitors each year, Haworth annually plays host to more than one million tourists and, overall, tourism is worth about £20 million to the local economy.

In order to further raise the profile of the region and to ensure that it increases its share of the tourism and leisure market, Brontë Country Tourism was launched as a marketing organisation in March 1996. Backed by the Keighley Business Forum and liaising with other local and regional tourism organisations, the overall aim of Brontë Country Tourism is to establish 'Brontë Country' as a readily identifiable area (see Figure 5.4) with the travel trade and tourists themselves and to market all eligible tourism businesses within the region under a single brand name.

In other words, the purpose of the initiative is not only to increase tourism in Haworth itself but also to enable the entire area to benefit from the internationally recognised Brontë label. There are a

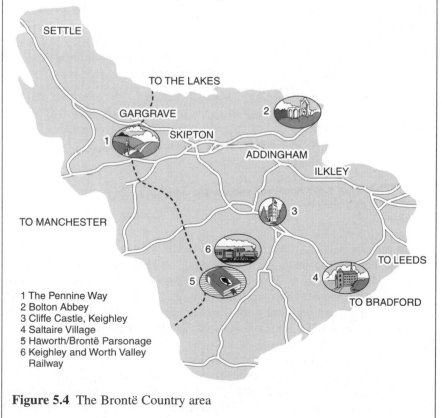

1 The Pennine Way
2 Bolton Abbey
3 Cliffe Castle, Keighley
4 Saltaire Village
5 Haworth/Brontë Parsonage
6 Keighley and Worth Valley
   Railway

Figure 5.4 The Brontë Country area

number of other tourist attractions in the region, including Bolton Abbey, the Keighley and Worth Valley steam railway and Saltaire 'model' village near Bradford, which are already popular, but which would undoubtedly benefit by being included under the 'Brontë Country' umbrella.

Membership of Brontë Country Tourism is, therefore, open to all businesses within the area's tourism sector, including transport operators, hotels and guest houses, shops, pubs and restaurants, and the organisation undertakes a variety of marketing activities on behalf of its membership. These include:

● attending exhibitions, such as the World Travel Market, at home and abroad;
● making targeted out-of-area presentations. During the first year of operations, presentations were made in South Africa and the United States as well as in the UK;
● hosting media and familiarisation visits. The BBC's 'Holiday Programme' and the Myrtle Beach, South Carolina, Chamber of Commerce visited during 1996;
● publishing a quarterly bulletin of events for the travel trade and media;
● marketing 'Brontë Country' on the Internet;
● developing and marketing short break holidays and other products, such as 'Brontë Country Breaks' organised with a local transport operator;
● advertising the area in travel trade and regional publications;
● creating and maintaining a travel trade database.

The success of Brontë Country Tourism can only be assessed in the longer term. Nevertheless, many of the activities already undertaken, in particular the development of international links, are evidence of the way in which the Brontë label can be successfuly used to promote an area to a wider audience.

Source: The authors gratefully acknowledge the help of Carolyn Spencer, Manager, Brontë Country Tourism, in compiling this case study.

Whilst any increase in tourism to rural areas as a result of such media exposure has, in the past, been incidental, tourist promotions using the name of a film, television show or author are now used to project the overall image, to reinforce the rural association and to encourage demand. Moreover, local and regional public sector organisations are now actively encouraging films and television shows to locate in their particular regions because of this spin-off effect.

However, this use of the countryside image as a promotional tool is not without its accompanying problems, particularly as appealing images often serve to oversell specific sites and inflate visitor expectations. Thus, an effective regional promotional campaign may generate increased awareness of, and tourism demand to, a certain area but, unless all the individual businesses involved have a professional approach to formulating and delivering their product offering, customer expectations will not be met. More generally, the rural image presented in, for example, a film may simply not exist in reality.

Therefore, the second important role of public sector organisations in rural tourism marketing, in addition to overall, or 'macro', image and promotional campaigns, is to support and guide product development and marketing at the micro level. In other words, the public sector, in the realisation that to channel resources into promotion and image whilst neglecting the product itself may lead to problems, is becomingly increasingly involved in working with individual tourism businesses through the process of marketing facilitation. The purpose of marketing facilitation is, generally, to help smaller rural tourism organisations to maximise their business opportunities and to ensure that the local or regional rural tourism industry works towards common objectives.

Normally, of course, public sector organisations are unable to directly *control* the activities of the private sector. Nevertheless, through marketing facilitation they are able to *influence* its product development and marketing efforts by providing guidance, leadership and, where necessary, direct support. This can be achieved through a variety of techniques, which may include:

- the provision of tourism information and statistics to fulfil small businesses' market research requirements;
- direct training and consultancy services for the private sector;
- representation at travel trade shows, which individual rural tourism businesses would not normally attend;
- the organisation of workshops for particular sectors of the industry;
- support with information production and distribution;
- the development and management of reservation systems which may be run, for example, by local or regional Tourism Information Centre networks;
- the provision of grants, preferential loans or other financial incentives for product development.

This list is by no means exhaustive (see, for example, Middleton 1988: 218–223) and the extent to which public sector organisations utilise different techniques or the range of services they offer will be dependent on their own objectives and scale of operations. Thus, a national tourism organisation is normally able to become more involved in marketing facilitation and to provide support and guidance in more ways than, say, a local chamber of commerce. Nevertheless, marketing facilitation is a vital function of public sector organisations and is likely to become more so as the rural tourism industry continues to grow and as an increasing number of destinations, facilities and attractions compete for a share of the rural tourism market.

PROBLEMS OF MARKETING RURAL TOURISM: MARKETING THE PLACE

Perhaps the greatest challenge in rural tourism marketing faced by those organisations with the responsibility of 'marketing an area' is not so much in getting the destination image right, or even in providing the means to help individual businesses improve their contribution to the overall tourism product (although these are both crucial to destination success). It is more in helping to create the *experience* that will satisfy the needs of the customer, the rural tourist.

Customer satisfaction is, generally, derived from the existence of key product benefits, such as relaxation or a sense of escape, which are provided, in part, by the tangible, or physical, features of the product, such as accommodation, attractions, scenery and so on. However, satisfaction also depends upon the intangible extras and features which add utility and enable tourists to experience not only the core benefits sought but also to feel that they are getting value for money. In the context of the rural tourism destination, these 'extras' may include, for example, the ease of access to and within the countryside or the availability of information and, together with the core products, they form the total rural tourism product to be marketed (see Figure 5.5)

There are a number of reasons, however, why it is difficult for organisations to bridge this gap between the benefits expected and the total product:

- The rural tourism product is largely assembled by and, therefore, unique to the individual tourist. As a result, the core product and benefits sought will be different in each case and, thus, destination agencies will always be attempting to market a product about which they have limited knowledge. For example, one tourist might be seeking the freedom and solitude of the open countryside whilst, for another, the countryside may merely be a pleasant setting for shopping at craft centres.
- Places are multi-sold and, therefore, visitors undertaking a variety of activities will impact upon each others enjoyment. As Ashworth and Voogt (1990) point out, 'multi-selling of the same physical

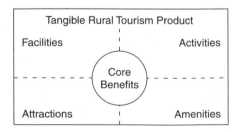

Figure 5.5 The total rural tourism product

space can result in precisely the same land use conflicts long famil-
iar to local authority planning departments'. This also means that
there is a need to provide for a range of experiences to satisfy the
customer.

- Those responsible for overall product augmentation and promotion are
rarely the same as those responsible for operation of the physical
product, often leading to problems of quality control and a lack of
co-operation between individual tourism businesses, even where this
would enhance the customer experience.

- The features which are or are not included in the marketing of the
overall tourism product will often depend upon the physical area
covered by local or regional government or, in the case of marketing
bureaux, upon which private enterprises have subscribed to that
area's marketing organisation. In other words, the organisational
view of the tourism product may by no means reflect the tourists'
perceptions of what should be included in that area product. Some
major marketing difficulties are, therefore, caused by the existence of
product 'boundaries'.

- 'Too often, within the public sector itself, agencies with overlapping
and competing responsibilities lead either to inaction or cross-purpose
actions' (Kotler *et al.* 1993: 42). It is, therefore, important that the
marketing efforts of public sector organisations are viewed within the
context of their wider roles and responsibilities.

In addition to these problems, there is also evidence to show that public
organisations, whilst keen to jump onto the tourism bandwagon,
frequently do not have the necessary marketing expertise to do so. For
example, Gilbert and Tung (1990) found that, within UK public sector
organisations involved in rural tourism, 'much of the work carried out by
public sector bodies is administered by managers without a formal
marketing training' and that, of those surveyed, 'less than a third were
found to have rural marketing policies'.

PROBLEMS OF MARKETING RURAL TOURISM: THE PRIVATE SECTOR

There is little doubt that, in the case of tourism businesses, marketing is
being under-utilised as a business tool. Indeed, it has been suggested that
'marketing is all too seldom applied in the business world, and still less in
the travel and tourism industry' (Holloway and Plant 1992: 3), an observation which is of particular relevance to rural tourism. For example, some
rural tourism businesses may have existed for many years and their managers will have been brought up 'in the business'; many, however, will have
evolved more recently from local farming, retail or catering trades. In both
cases, management techniques may be in place which appear to work well
but which, in the absence of a systematic approach to marketing and
management, may mean that the business is not realising its full potential.

There are, of course exceptions, in particular amongst the larger rural tourism organisations. For example, Country Holidays is the largest supplier of rented rural holiday accommodation in the UK and, as part of the international Thomson group, is resourced with a wealth of marketing expertise. However, the rural tourism industry is mostly comprised of small, often family-run businesses, and these smaller organisations have tended not to undertake marketing for a number of reasons:

- There is a general lack of understanding of the principles of marketing and its potential benefits to a small business, especially in relation to the perceived financial outlay involved. For example, the purchase of tourism market intelligence, consultancy or membership of a marketing bureau is often expensive in relation to the tourism turnover of a rural organisation, especially when tourism is seen as a by-product of other main income-earning activities, such as farming.
- In many areas it is difficult for small enterprises to finance a new marketing approach; because 'banks are hesitant about the small-scale structure of rural tourism, they don't want to invest small amounts of capital in many different projects' (Hummelbrunner and Miglbauer 1994). Moreover, whilst there may be opportunities to secure a loan on a larger scale, community basis, it is may be difficult to encourage a number of local, competing organisations to work together.
- In many rural communities there is very often a suspicion of, and unwillingness to accept, the ideas and advice of 'outsiders'. Ideas generated from within the community setting appear to be more acceptable than those imposed from outside (see Chapter 6) but, even where local information and advice is available, businesses have to be encouraged to use it.

MARKETING RURAL TOURISM: A STRUCTURED APPROACH

This chapter has emphasised the fact that all public and private sector organisations need to adopt a more positive approach to marketing in order to develop and manage a successful rural tourism industry in what is becoming an increasingly dynamic and competitive tourism environment. However, a number of general problems have been highlighted which, it is suggested, may hinder the development of a co-ordinated approach to the marketing of rural tourism.

In many countries, much of the day to day responsibility for managing the rural tourism product and its components lies with the private sector and, arguably, it is at this level that there is a pressing need for the development of, and improvements in, the marketing process. However, rural economies in most OECD countries do not yet have a private sector which is sufficiently developed to achieve this on its own and, because of long-term structural weaknesses, it is unlikely that this position will change in the near future (OECD 1994). Therefore, it is evident that the public sector has an important role to play in encouraging and stimulating the development of marketing.

One of the most widely advocated methods of involving the public sector in tourism marketing is through the development of partnerships with the private sector and other relevant organisations (see Chapter 6). There are a number of problems inherent in this approach, particularly with respect to overall control, funding and the co-ordination of interests. There are also questions as to how long and the extent to which the public sector should be involved and indeed, whether or not such involvement can achieve the aim of enabling the private sector to operate in the long run without public sector support. In other words, the main issue is not if, but *how* public sector involvement should be established.

There is however, no common agreement as to the structure of public/private sector partnerships and the resulting role of the public sector, and, in some areas, 'co-operatives, semi-state agencies and private consultancies carry out roles reserved elsewhere for the state sector' (OECD 1994: 41). Nevertheless, it has been suggested that 'it is not a question of selecting *one* single structure, but of the proper combination of structures and organisations at different levels and with different tasks' (Hummelbrunner and Miglbauer 1994). They propose a three-tier approach, comprising local and regional tourism organisations which would bring together individual operators in joint marketing initiatives, local support structures to provide training, advice and information, and top-down support, whereby local tourism products are marketed on the national and international stage.

As the following case study demonstrates, this approach has been successfully implemented in Austria and, although relating specifically to farm tourism, it nevertheless provides a general model for the development of public/private sector rural tourism marketing schemes. Inevitably, the applicability of this model is subject to regional or national differences, and its long-term success will not be known for a number of years.

Case study 9: Farm tourism in Austria

Farm tourism in Austria is not a new phenomenon; in fact, about a quarter of all Austrian farms have been receiving tourists for almost a century (Hummelbrunner and Miglbauer 1994). However, it is only in recent years that the need for a positive approach to marketing has been recognised and, for a number of reasons, a concerted effort has been made to organise the representation and marketing of farm, or agricultural, tourism in a more professional way:

● Agri-tourism plays a key role in the Austrian tourism industry. Accommodation on farms represents about 18 per cent of the total supply of tourist beds in Austria, equating to 21,000 farmers offering some 109,000 rooms (including bedrooms in apartments). Moreover, 10 per cent of all farmers in Austria supply farmhouse holidays as a means of earning a secure income (Pichler 1991).

- The level of bookings for overnight stays has been in decline for a number of years and, in 1992, the trend appeared set to continue. The number of small enterprises (with up to ten bedrooms) involved in farm tourism also significantly decreased during the 1980s.
- In 1992, the average occupancy rate for farm accommodation was just 15 per cent, or 54 days, per year, whilst 80 to 100 days per year is commonly regarded as a minimum viable letting period.
- The characteristics of potential rural tourists in Austria have been changing. Traditionally, farm holidays were popular as a cheap form of accommodation but, as in many other countries, rural tourism is now attracting a new, better-off clientele.

The first attempts to co-ordinate the marketing of farm accommodation in Austria did not take place until the early 1970s when a group of farmers in the Salzkammergut – a tourist region in the provinces of Salzburg and Upper Austria – began to pool their promotional efforts. Between 1972 and 1992 a number of provincial Farm Holidays Associations were established but it became clear that, unless farm-based holidays were to become just one of the many products promoted by the existing tourism framework in Austria, farmers would have to begin to play a more active role in the development of farm tourism from the local to the national level. Therefore, it was decided that a national organisation would be needed to promote and co-ordinate farm holidays throughout the country and, in 1991, eight provinces joined forces to create the Austrian Farm Holidays Association (Bundesverband für Urlaub am Bauernhof in Österreich) to oversee a four-tier organisational structure (individual farmers, local groups of farmers, provincial associations and, at the federal level, the national Association) to promote farm holidays on a regional, provincial and national basis.

The main objectives of creating the national organisational network were to:

- optimise the opportunities for agricultural enterprises to develop tourism;
- include farm holidays as an essential feature of Austria's tourism product;
- improve Austria's competitive position within the European market, in particular in terms of quality, variety and creativity;
- organise product marketing in such a way that farms offering farm holidays would be given a fighting chance in the market for holidays in general.

The overall purpose of the Austrian Farm Holidays Association is to act as a motivator for farmers wishing to offer farm holidays and to be the recognisable contact for farmers, guests and all other relevant organisations. It also works towards establishing recognised quality standards amongst its member farms.

Each organisational tier has specific objectives within the overall marketing strategies of the network as a whole (Table 5.2)

Overall marketing strategies

The overall marketing strategies of the Association are designed, in general to develop and promote links between potential customers and individual farms, individuality and personal contact being considered the major strengths of the farm tourism product. In order to achieve this, the Association's marketing strategies include:

- the development of a classification system (using a 'flower' mark) to ensure uniform standards;
- improving co-operation with existing tourism organisations;
- the creation of a uniform corporate identity and image for all farm holidays;
- helping farmers to differentiate their product for specific target groups;
- an emphasis on regional, rather than national, characteristics, with farms promoted in provincial brochures only;

Table 5.2 Objectives of organisational levels

Level 1–Farmers	Farmers, as landlords, have the task of providing a good quality tourist product to a guaranteed standard, providing precise information for guests and willingly co-operating with the requirements of the Farm Holidays scheme.
Level 2–Regional groups	At the regional level, pools or 'guest circles' are required to organise a booking system, training, consultancy and advice for farmers, and an opportunity for farmers to exchange experiences. They are also required to assist provincial associations at the regional level.
Level 3–Provincial associations	The responsibilities of the eight provincial associations include optimising marketing at all levels, organising a provincial-level booking scheme and liaising with other provincial level tourism organisations, chambers of agriculture, provincial government and with the federal level.
Level 4–National association	The objectives of the Austrian Farm Holidays Association itself include: overseeing national and international promotion and marketing; lobbying in the interests of farm holidays; maintaining contacts with national bodies, such as the Austrian National Tourist Office and the Federal Ministry of Agriculture; and manning a central information office for farm holidays in Austria.

Source: adapted from Embacher (1994)

- raising prices in line with higher quality standards but with prices geared towards the family market;
- the improvement of product promotion and distribution through co-operation with travel agencies and transport operators;
- public relations and market research activities.

Finances

The Farm Holiday Associations receive financial support from a number of private and public sector sources, including farmers' membership fees, Chambers of Agriculture (which, in most cases, provide office space for the Provincial Associations), the Ministry of Agriculture and Forestry and from regional, provincial and national tourism organisations. The latter organisations also provide support through the production of promotional materials and representation at trade fairs.

Information and training

Training is provided both for Association staff and for farmers. It includes training in marketing and sales, public relations, guest correspondence and other specific skills. Seminars and regular discussion sessions are also organised and farmers are required to pay a small contribution towards the costs of training. Association staff training is subsidised by the Ministry of Agriculture and Forestry and the Chambers of Agriculture.

Although farm tourism in Austria has been popular for many years, tourists' needs are changing and the overall market for national and international holidays is much more competitive. Today's tourists are looking for a much more 'intelligent' product (Embacher 1994), requiring a professional and co-ordinated approach. The creation of a strong 'Farm Holidays' brand through the work of the Austrian Farm Holidays Association not only reassures these potential farm guests of the quality of their holiday, but it will also serve to strengthen the position Austrian farm accommodation within the European market, particularly in the face of increasing competition from rural tourism developments in eastern European countries.

The evolution of the Farm Holiday Association network has also helped to highlight the difficulties faced by all small rural tourism operators. On their own, they lack the management and marketing expertise, as well as financial resources, necessary to meet the needs of the changing consumer. The structure of the Farm Holidays Association, however, enables farmers to benefit from a level and quality of marketing normally associated with larger commercial organisations whilst retaining their independence and individual identity. The scheme has also been successful; since 1991, the number of bed nights booked on Austrian farms has increased considerably.

CONCLUSION

Marketing is not an activity normally associated with the rural tourism industry. At the private sector level, dominated by a large number of small businesses, most organisations lack the financial resources, expertise or, perhaps, willingness to become involved in marketing on an individual basis whilst, at the public sector level, rural tourism marketing has not, traditionally, been a priority for agencies, such as forestry organisations or agricultural advisory services, involved in rural development.

However, as greater emphasis is placed on the role of tourism as a means of regenerating rural areas and as the tourism market itself becomes more competitive on a local, national and international scale, there is, as this chapter suggests, a pressing need for an approach more focused on marketing at all levels of the rural tourism industry. For example, as Slee and Yells (1984/85) argue, if the farm tourism sector is to realise its economic potential, 'a more conscious adoption of the principles of marketing will be a necessity'.

To achieve this, a number of hurdles need to be overcome and recent experience has demonstrated that the establishment of structured, effective partnerships provides a firm basis for the development of co-ordinated marketing strategies. Nevertheless, further research needs to be undertaken to monitor the viability of different structures and approaches which may be appropriate to different rural tourism settings. Fundamental to this is a recognition of the essential role of marketing in the overall rural tourism planning and management process.

QUESTIONS

1. Consider within the context of rural tourism the proposition that the principles and techniques of marketing can be applied to any organisation in any industry.
2. Explain and give examples of the problems facing the public and private sectors in the marketing of rural tourism.
3. Why is it necessary for public sector rural tourism marketing organisations to concentrate on both overall image promotion and marketing facilitation?
4. Consider and give examples of the benefits and disadvantages of rural tourism marketing campaigns based upon literary and/or media associations.

FURTHER READING

Ashworth, G. and Goodall, B. (1990) *Marketing Tourism Places*, London: Routledge.

Holloway, J. C. and Robinson, C. (1995) *Marketing for Tourism*, London: Pitman Publishing.

Kotler, P., Haider, D. and Rein, I. (1993) *Marketing Places*, New York: Free Press.

Middleton, V. (1994) *Marketing in Travel and Tourism,* 2nd edition, Oxford: Heinemann.

Seaton, A. and Bennett, M. (1996) *Marketing Tourism Products: Concepts, Issues, Cases*, London: Chapman & Hall.

Planning and managing rural tourism

6

INTRODUCTION

Since the early 1980s, rural areas in many industrialised countries have been greatly affected by structural changes occurring in national and regional economies. Few, if any, areas have escaped the problems of population decline, falling levels of employment and income, diminishing public services and the loss of rural identity and culture and, as a result, it is widely accepted that new strategies are required to assist the economic and social regeneration of rural communities (Holland and Crotts 1992). In particular, policy makers and planners have increasingly been looking to tourism as a 'potential industry force that may bring both economic and demographic stability to . . . rural communities' (Potts *et al.* 1992); the development of tourism is regarded by many as the solution to a number of the problems facing rural areas and is considered an essential ingredient of what has been described as the 'rural revitalization movement' (Kieselbach and Long 1990).

However, this growing emphasis and, in many instances, reliance upon tourism as a means of maintaining and regenerating rural communities has not, by and large, been matched by the formulation and implementation of proactive policies for the development and management of rural tourism. That is, although tourism has existed in many rural areas for well over a century and in some regions has long been a primary source of income and employment, there has been a surprising absence of positive planning for the provision and integration of tourism within broader rural development policies (Pigram 1993). Efforts that have been made to plan for rural tourism have generally been reactive, responding to the pressures and demands of tourism, and have typically been focused on the perceived need to manage and, in effect, contain rural recreational activities rather than to promote them positively. This approach, concentrating on issues such as visitor controls and environmental conservation, is important within the context of visitor management in the countryside but it is limited inasmuch as it fails to address the wider economic and social implications of rural tourism development (OECD 1994). It is also interesting to note that, despite the existence of a number of detailed texts concerned with tourism planning in general (for example, see Inskeep 1991; Gunn 1994; WTO 1994), the specific issue of rural tourism management has, until recently, been largely overlooked within the tourism literature.

There are, of course, exceptions. For example, in 1989 the National Policy Study on Rural Tourism and Small Businesses was undertaken in the United States under the auspices of the United States Travel and Tourism Administration (USTTA). Based on six months extensive research, the study concluded that a specific need for a federal policy on rural tourism development existed and it recommended that tourism should be recognised as a valid and important element of rural economic development. Similarly, in France it was recognised that, as rural tourism represents about 25 per cent of all French tourism, a national strategy for rural tourism was required. As a result, 'L'Association Tourisme en Éspace Rural' (TER) was established during the 1980s to co-ordinate the development of the French rural tourism product (see Cointat 1991). This organisation has evolved into EUROTER, the European rural tourism organisation sponsored by the Council of Europe. More recently, the Department of Tourism in Australia also published a strategy document for rural tourism, examining how both the industry and the government can contribute to the growth of rural tourism through considered planning, development and management (ADT 1994).

There are also many examples of more local initiatives designed to plan and manage the integrated and balanced development of tourism in rural areas, concentrating in particular on the issues of sustainable tourism and community based tourism development. Furthermore, a number of tourism organisations and related agencies have produced policy statements which refer to the development and promotion of rural tourism. Nevertheless, there still remains a 'policy implementation gap' (Pigram 1993) between the recognition of the potential benefits of tourism in rural areas and the practical integration of tourism into rural development plans. Therefore, this chapter examines the need for the effective management and planning of rural tourism and considers a number of related issues and challenges. In particular, it highlights the need for a comprehensive and integrated approach to the development of rural tourism and in so doing it brings together many of the issues raised throughout this book.

THE NEED FOR PLANNING AND MANAGEMENT

There is little doubt that the effective and co-ordinated planning and management of rural tourism is a complex task. As the preceding chapters have shown, not only is the demand for rural tourism diverse, encompassing an enormous variety of activities which depend upon or utilise a wide range of attractions and environments, but also that demand is generally informal, spontaneous and, by implication, difficult to manage or influence. The supply of rural tourism is equally diverse; natural or man-made attractions, amenities and facilities, marketing and information services and transport are all tangible elements of the rural tourism product, yet the intrinsic qualities of the rural environment, such as a sense of space, peace and tranquillity, or a place to escape from the modern world, are also vital ingredients of rural tourism but, again, difficult to control. Furthermore, the countryside is a multi-purpose resource. Tourism is just one of a number of competing demands on the countryside and it is suggested that tourism is frequently considered to be a 'challenge and even a threat to established modes of productive resource use' (Pigram 1993:156). In short, two notable features of rural tourism are, first, the fragmented and diverse character of both demand and supply and, second, the dynamic and variable claims upon its resource base. Together, they complicate the planning and management process and, perhaps, go some way to explaining the general lack of rural tourism development policies, whilst some might take the extreme view that, ultimately, the tourism industry as a whole is unmanageable.

However, it may be argued that a systematic and integrated approach to the planning and management of rural tourism is both justifiable and necessary for a number of reasons. Generally, an interdependence exists between all the components of rural tourism destinations; it is the physical and socio-cultural attributes of rural areas that attract tourists and which are the resource base for the tourism industry, yet tourism is also increasingly contributing to the maintenance of those attributes. Therefore, careful planning is required to ensure that a balance is achieved between satisfying the needs of tourists, the tourism industry and local rural communities. Table 6.1 summarises the various inter-related components of rural tourism destinations that require consideration in any rural tourism development plan.

More specifically, it can be argued that the development of rural tourism should be carefully planned and managed for the following reasons:

● The decline of farming and agriculture as the dominant land use in rural areas and the increasing diversity of demands placed upon the

Table 6.1 Components of rural tourism destinations

Physical	Economic	Socio-cultural
living resources	employment	government
non-living resources	income	history
	taxes	architecture
		education
	Impacts	
air	employment	public safety
water	infrastructure	aesthetic
geological	cost of living	human services
flora and fauna		folk culture
		social structure
	Major issues	
conservation	stability	sense of peace
enhancement	investment	quality of life
pollution	diversity	social involvement

Source: Potts *et al.* 1992

countryside means that overall policies are required to determine the effective allocation of rural resources to appropriate uses, including tourism.

- It is generally accepted that tourism can be an appropriate and beneficial vehicle for the economic and social revitalisation of rural areas (Dernoi 1991). However, given the fragmented and typically small-scale character of the rural tourism industry, broader and longer-term planning and guidance is needed to ensure that the benefits to local communities are optimised.

- The countryside is a fragile resource which is highly susceptible to environmental and social change. Therefore, there is a limit to the nature and scale of tourism that any particular rural area can absorb depending on its physical and socio-cultural characteristics. It is vital that these characteristics and qualities which attract visitors in the first place are not degraded or lost as a result of excessive or inappropriate tourism development, and this can only be achieved through continual management of both the industry and of tourists themselves.

- It has been suggested that tourism has developed into an established and mature industry (OECD 1994). Tourists have greater expectations of choice and quality, whilst the industry itself is gradually recognising that it has a longer-term responsibility towards the environment within which it operates. Arguably, this responsibility is most acute within rural areas where the development of tourism is irrevocably linked to the health of the environment, and it can only be met through effective planning and management.

Overall, then, it is evident that a considered and strategic approach to planning and management is required if the development of tourism is to optimise the benefits both to rural areas and to tourists whilst being 'consistent with the limitations imposed by social and environmental conditions of the destination area' (Holland and Crotts 1992). Inevitably, however, the policies and aims of tourism development will vary according to these local conditions and, therefore, there is no universal or ideal method of implementing plans and policies that is applicable to all situations. Nevertheless, the initial planning process is likely to be similar in most, if not all, situations.

RURAL TOURISM: THE PLANNING AND MANAGEMENT PROCESS

'Planning tourism at all levels is essential for achieving successful tourism development' (WTO 1994). Experience has shown that, where tourism has been allowed to evolve in a haphazard, unplanned fashion, environmental and social problems can emerge which, in the longer-term, may outweigh the potential benefits of tourism. That is, the unrestrained and unmanaged development of tourism can easily diminish the attraction of a destination to the extent that tourists no longer wish to go there, with serious economic and social consequences for local communities (Holloway 1994: 253). In short, unplanned tourism can be a self-destructive process.

Increasing concern about the negative impacts of tourism mirrored the rapid growth of mass tourism during the 1970s (Young 1973; Turner and Ash 1975; de Kadt 1979) and, since then, much research has been undertaken into the impacts of tourism development, both generally and also in relation to specific destinations, regions, or forms of tourism. Similarly, attention has increasingly been focused upon finding solutions to the problems of tourism development. Interestingly, it was the impacts of tourism in the Alpine region of Europe (one of the first popular rural tourism destinations) that led to the emergence of alternative proposals for tourism development (see Krippendorf 1987; Smith and Eadington 1992) and concepts such as alternative, responsible, soft, appropriate or green tourism were proposed as means of reducing the negative impacts of tourism. During the 1990s, reflecting the more general growth in environmental awareness and concern, these ideas have evolved into a broader perspective on tourism planning and the principals of sustainable tourism development have become more widely accepted.

The specific issue of planning for sustainable tourism is one of considerable debate amongst both tourism academics and practitioners, and it is considered in more detail later in this chapter. However, the important point here is that it is not the end result of tourism planning that is of concern, but the means or process by which that end result is achieved. In other words, the purpose of planning and managing rural tourism is, generally, to 'balance demand and capacity so that conflicts are minimised and the countryside is used to its full potential without deterioration of the resource base' (Pigram 1993: 171). The question is, through what process can that balance be achieved?

As a starting point, Fagence (1991) suggests that there are a number of common characteristics and roles of rural tourism development that may be used to focus the planning and management process:

- Tourism can be an effective means of regenerating rural areas as long as it is a catalyst for wider economic diversification, or one of a number of sources of economic stimulation.
- Any tourism development policy should be integrated into broader development strategies.
- Tourism may be used as a catalyst or justification for infrastructural, transport and public service improvements in rural areas.
- On a regional basis, the most effective form of rural tourism development is one based upon 'locational specialisation and intraregional complementarity'.
- Not all local tourism businesses will directly benefit the local community, particularly when outside interests become involved in the development of tourism.
- Visitors to rural areas are no less demanding than tourists in urban or coastal locations and thus demand a wide variety of types and quality of attractions and facilities.

From the above, it is evident that, despite the different contexts in which rural tourism occurs, there are common issues and problems to address. Thus, all rural tourism planning can, arguably, be based upon a logical and strategic process to ensure optimal outcomes. Inherent in this process should be the recognition of the particular susceptibility of rural areas and communities to the potential social and environmental costs of tourism development described in Chapter 2 and all rural tourism development policies should, therefore, be guided by the need to be 'host sensitive' (Holland and Crotts 1992). Table 6.2 illustrates a tourism planning and management process which is applicable to most rural tourism planning situations and which is explained in the following sections. Reference may also be made to Dowling (1993), Long (1993), and Gunn (1994: 142).

Setting objectives

The first stage of any rural tourism planning process must be the determination of the objectives of developing tourism. These objectives are, in effect, a statement of the desired outcomes of developing tourism in a rural area or destination and may include a wide range of aims, such as job creation or retention, economic diversification, the support of public services, the conservation or redevelopment of traditional buildings and, of course, the provision of recreational opportunities for tourists. The objectives should normally take into account broader regional or national development objectives and, as part of a continual cycle, be reviewed as a result of the completion of the following stages of the planning process.

Table 6.2 The rural tourism planning and management process

Stages	Processes
1. Setting objectives	Determination of objectives Comparison of objectives Integration with broader plans and objectives
2. Surveys	Quantitative data (patterns, trends) Qualitative data Socio-economic, political, environmental factors
3. Analysis and synthesis	Evaluation of survey data Combined analysis of all data Projection of requirements, capacities
4. Proposals	Preparation of alternative plans Selection of most appropriate policies
5. Implementation and management	Continual process of: – implementation – monitoring – evaluation

Source: adapted from WTO (1994)

Surveys and research

The second stage of the planning process comprises research into all relevant aspects of tourism and the proposed development area. These include factors such as the physical and socio-cultural characteristics of the destination area, economic and employment patterns, existing and planned infrastructure, rural tourism patterns and trends, existing and planned tourist attractions and facilities, competitive attractions and destinations in the region, private and public sector organisations working directly or indirectly in tourism, and so on. (See Figure 6.1 for a more complete list of research requirements). Of particular importance, especially in the context of sustainable rural tourism development, is research into the attitudes of local residents towards the development of tourism.

Surveys have shown that the attitudes towards tourism development can vary amongst members of host communities, indicating the necessity of including local communities in the planning process. (See, for example, Pizam 1978; Brougham and Butler 1981; Perdue *et al.* 1987; Liu *et al.* 1987.)

Effective and in-depth surveys are essential in order to identify potential tourism development areas. As Gunn (1994: 143) points out, a present fallacious belief is that all areas possess equal potential for tourism development and that 'with greater expenditures on advertising, any area can enjoy the fruits of tourism'. On the contrary, many rural areas are unsuitable for tourism development and characteristics such as ease of access from large conurbations or scenic value do not guarantee success (OECD 1994). Furthermore, as the following case study on rural tourism

---

Figure 6.1 Components of tourism planning surveys

- Global, regional and local tourism patterns and trends.
- Characteristics of similar existing or potential rural tourism destinations in the region with similar products, attractions and markets.
- Tourist arrival trends in the proposed development area, including numbers and characteristics of tourist arrivals.
- Existing and potential tourist attractions and activities.
- Existing and planned tourist accommodation and other facilities and services.
- Existing and planned transport services both to and within the region.
- Other types of existing or planned infrastructure.
- Existing natural resources and patterns of land ownership and land use.
- Existing economic and employment patterns, including employment in tourism.
- Physical and social development plans.
- Environmental characteristics and environmental quality, including weather patterns, geographical characteristics, air and water quality, levels of pollution, etc.
- Socio-cultural patterns.
- Existing and planned education and training programmes, including tourism training and courses at educational institutions.
- Existing public and private sector organisations directly and indirectly involved in tourism in the region.
- Existing investment policies and the availability of capital for investment in tourism facilities.
- Existing tourism policy and legislation.

Source: adapted from WTO (1994)

in Romania shows (Case study 9), a number of barriers exist which may actually restrict the development of tourism in rural areas.

Case study 10: Rural tourism development in Transylvania, Romania

Tourism is not a new phenomenon in Romania. It has long been a winter sports destination for overseas visitors, there are a number of established resorts along the Black Sea coast playing host to both domestic tourists and visitors from neighbouring countries, and the country's spectacular scenery and rich cultural heritage have attracted tourists for many years (Turnock 1991). However, in common with many other former Eastern bloc countries, increasing emphasis has been placed upon the development of tourism since the collapse of the old regimes. Faced with significant economic, social and political problems and change, yet benefiting from a wealth of natural and cultural attractions, tourism has been seen as the obvious choice as a tool for economic and social regeneration and diversification with rural areas, in particular, being targeted for tourism development. In fact, in 1993 the Romanian Government initiated a reform programme which included objectives for tourism development and, in 1994, the legal framework was established for the national development of rural tourism.

However, despite this official support and the undoubted potential for a thriving tourism industry, there are a number of barriers to the successful development of tourism in rural areas in Romania, even in those regions, such as the one described here, which possess perhaps the greatest potential for tourism. Undoubtedly, some of these problems stem from the historical development of the Romanian countryside and it is important to outline this briefly before looking at the specific challenges facing rural tourism development in the Bran area of Transylvania.

Rural policies in Romania The countryside, with its communities, has always been at the heart of Romanian culture (Turnock 1990) and, until the 1950s, Romania was essentially an agrarian society. However, under the Ceaucescu regime, agriculture became completely state-controlled with 95 per cent of arable land being taken into State ownership. The production and distribution of crops and livestock was controlled by the Ministry of Agriculture and Food Industries with much production earmarked for export and, as a result of centralised planning and control, employment in agriculture fell dramatically. By 1991, for example, agriculture represented just 27.5 per cent of total employment, compared with 75 per cent of total employment in the post Second World War years. Rural populations were moved to industrial centres, agriculture and rural areas were starved of resources and investment and, generally, traditional rural economies and societies almost disappeared.

Since 1990, the restoration of Romania's rural economic and social systems has been seen as a priority, not only to ensure an adequate food supply at the local level but also to contribute to the cultural renaissance of rural areas. Some 80 per cent of sequestrated land has been returned to private ownership and, although production fell initially as a result of this reorganisation, output levels have been increasing in recent years as a result of the agricultural sector becoming dominated by larger, more economically managed farms. The effect of the agricultural reform policy has, however, been to perpetuate the out-migration of people from rural areas and, therefore, attention has been increasingly focused on tourism as a means of both regenerating rural economies through farm diversification and of maintaining and restoring Romania's vanishing agrarian culture.

Rural tourism in Bran, Transylvania One such area where tourism development has become a priority is the Bran region of Transylvania (see Figure 6.2) in central Romania. The area, covering almost 200 square kilometres and comprising twelve villages, is centred upon the main village of Bran. Originally established as a trading post between Transylvania and Wallachia, the village itself is well known for its castle which, built in 1377, is a popular tourist attraction (owing partly to its unsubstantiated links with Bram Stoker's Count Dracula), whilst the surrounding countryside has long been a popular tourist destination, particularly for Romanians wishing to escape the summer heat of Bucharest.

In one sense, the area is typical of the region in terms of landscape and lack of infrastructural development but, in other respects, it is unusual. First, it has always been a relatively wealthy area as a result of its strategic trading position, second, the land, being mountainous and, hence, unsuitable for arable farming, escaped nationalisation and, finally,

Figure 6.2 Map of Romania

alternative employment has been available in nearby towns, minimising out-migration from the area. Thus, not only have local householders been able to afford the conversion or extension of their homes to provide tourist accommodation, but also there is a tradition of tourism, albeit largely domestic, in the area. It was for these reasons that the Bran area was the basis of early developments in rural tourism when, in 1990, local people were permitted, for the first time in decades, to accommodate foreigners in their homes. More recently, rural tourism development in the area has been supported by the National Association of Rural, Ecological and Cultural Tourism (ANTREC) which works with a local company in Bran to promote tourism, to take reservations for accommodation, to develop training programmes, and so on.

However, despite the head-start enjoyed by the Bran area in developing rural tourism, a number of barriers to the future development of tourism have emerged. Over 70 per cent of visitors to the area are Romanian, whilst the majority of overseas visitors are on day trips from Brasov and, therefore, spend little time or money in the villages. Thus, a major challenge is to promote the increasing stock of local accommodation to the overseas market, an activity which is dependent on the support of national organisations such as ANTREC. The accessibility of the region also represents a difficulty to visitors, particularly foreign independent tourists. Other identified problems are:

- Little or no training is available to help local people develop and present the tourist product to foreign visitors.
- Perceptions of what overseas visitors need are often at variance with actual requirements. For example, much farmhouse accommodation for foreigners 'boasts' modern furniture and satellite television, facilities which are likely to be at odds with what many overseas visitors to rural areas expect, or even wish, to experience.
- Rural hosts have been found to be too attentive, eager to please and anxious to communicate with their guests, making many visitors feel uncomfortable.

More generally, mirroring the situation in other rural areas in Romania, other barriers to tourism development include:

- The unwillingness or inability of local people, having lived for many years under an oppressive regime, to take the initiative in business development.
- A tendency to exploit (or 'rip off') tourists, putting short-term profit before the longer term development of a tourism industry based on fairness and honesty.
- A recognised lethargy amongst the workforce, resulting in the tourism industry being unable to match or exceed the service provided by rural tourism operators in other countries.

Most of these problems result from cultural differences between overseas visitors and their Romanian hosts, differences which, given time, should be surmountable. Nevertheless, they demonstrate that, even in a rural area with a variety of attractions, a unique culture and a good supply of accommodation, the successful planning and development of rural tourism can be frustrated not only by a lack of investment, but also by a lack of communication, training and national support.

Source: The authors gratefully acknowledge the help of Lesley Roberts, Newcastle College, UK, in the compilation of this case study. See also Roberts (1996).

Analysis and synthesis

Once the surveys have been completed, the next stage of the planning process is to evaluate the research findings. The results of each component of the survey are analysed separately and then combined to produce a more comprehensive and detailed evaluation of the potential for tourism development. Through this process of synthesis it should be possible to project, for example, the optimal number of tourists in relation to the carrying capacity of the region (the carrying capacity being the level of use that the countryside can sustain without the landscape, the well-being and prosperity of local communities or the enjoyment of visitors being degraded) and the facilities, services and recreational opportunities required to fulfil the income and employment needs of the community.

Proposals and recommendations

It is only at this stage that the plans and policies for tourism development are prepared. Ideally, a variety of ideas and concepts are considered resulting in the formulation of a number of alternative development proposals. These are then assessed against different factors, such as the extent to which they meet the stated objectives of tourism development or their potential for minimising the negative impacts on the local community and, based upon this evaluation, the optimal plans and policies are selected and recommendations made. Gunn (1994) suggests that these recommendations should be based on four aspects of tourism development:

- *Physical development* – the aim of which is to match the supply of attractions, facilities, opportunities and services with projected demand.
- *Programme development* – including recommendations for the provision of tourist information and promotional and marketing programmes.
- *Policies* – providing the framework for the integrated development of tourism in the area, including the rationale for, and means of achieving, the objectives of tourism development and the roles of all organisations and individuals concerned.
- *Priorities* – all recommendations should be reviewed and prioritised according to ease of implementation and the expected benefits of development.

Implementation and management

This final stage of the planning and management of rural tourism is, in fact, a continual process. The recommended plans are acted upon and the results of development continuously monitored in order to assess the extent to which the objectives and overall policies are being achieved. Ideally, this evaluation should include surveys of visitor satisfaction, measurement of the economic benefits to the local community, and ongoing environmental and socio-cultural impact assessment. Where necessary, policies may be adapted and management procedures initiated, for example vehicle or visitor controls, and, overall, the development of tourism should be monitored to ensure that it is commensurate with broader regional or national rural development policies.

As stated earlier, the objectives and policies of rural tourism development vary from one area to another. For example, in popular, established rural destinations, such as many of the national parks in the UK, conservation of the physical and socio-cultural environment has become of paramount importance and tourism development plans have been adapted accordingly to manage and control tourism. Conversely, many other rural areas, such as parts of eastern Europe, have enormous, untapped potential but, frequently lacking even the most basic infrastructure, face a completely different set of problems and challenges For example, Szabo (1991) and Balogh and Csaky (1991) respectively assess the potential for rural tourism in Romania and Hungary.

It has been suggested (Hummelbrunner and Miglbauer 1994) that there are three separate and identifiable contexts in relation to rural tourism planning, namely:

- Rural areas with a tradition in tourism development;
- Rural areas with little tradition in, but great potential for, tourism development;
- Rural areas with little or no tradition in tourism and only average development potential.

In each case, different strategies and inputs are required but there are a number of common key issues and questions which deserve attention, and it is to these that the remainder of this chapter is devoted.

SUSTAINABLE RURAL TOURISM DEVELOPMENT

'Sustainable tourism is a positive approach intended to reduce tensions and friction caused by the complex interactions between the tourism industry, visitors, the environment and the communities which are host to holiday makers' (Bramwell and Lane 1993). It is also an approach to tourism development which is, arguably, of particular relevance in rural areas, where the interdependency between tourism and the environment is most evident. However, despite the current attention being paid to sustainable tourism and, indeed, widespread acceptance of its principles, there is still much debate about the viability and even the meaning of sustainable development within the context of tourism (Butler 1990, 1992; Wheeller 1992a, 1992b; Burns and Holden 1995).

The origins of sustainable tourism lie in the emergence of proposals for alternative forms of tourism development in Europe during the early 1980s, which suggested ways of avoiding many of the problems and highly publicised negative impacts of conventional, mass tourism. At the same time, the more general concept of sustainable development was being debated on the international stage and in 1987 the World Commission on Environment and Development published its report, *Our Common Future*, in which it defined sustainable development as 'development that meets the needs of the present without compromising the ability of future generations to meet their own needs' (WCED 1987). In other words, sustainable development is 'about taking a long term view of the impact of development on the environment and the world's resources, and it is concerned with stewardship, good husbandry and equity' (Beioley 1995) or, more simply, ensuring that any economic activity, including tourism, has 'the capacity for continuance' (Porritt 1995).

Since the publication of *Our Common Future* (WCED 1987) and the 1992 Earth Summit in Rio de Janeiro, increasing numbers of organisations and industries at the international, national and local level and in both the public and private sectors have adopted the principles of sustainable development. Similarly, within tourism, sustainability has been embraced by planners, practitioners and academics as a positive principle for development, and there has been an ever-increasing flow of policy documents, planning guidelines and examples of good practice from a variety of sources. For example, the World Tourism Organisation has published a guide to sustainable tourism development (WTO 1993) and many national or local tourism organisations have done likewise.

Essentially, the basis of sustainable tourism development is recognition of the relationship that exists between the three components of the tourism operating environment, namely tourists, the destination environment and the host community (see Figure 6.3).

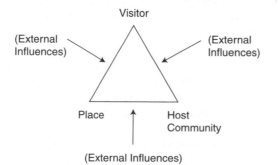

Figure 6.3 The tourism environment
Source: ETB/DoE (1991)

This relationship is both complex and dynamic, and can be both positive and negative. On the one hand, tourism can regenerate local economies, providing employment and income, it can contribute to the strengthening of local culture and it can be the catalyst for the conservation or renovation of the natural and man-made environment. On the other hand, tourism can also distort the local economy or degrade the environment and the quality of life of local communities. Thus, the objective of sustainable tourism is to maintain a harmonious balance between these three components whilst protecting the resource base in the longer term. This can be achieved, it is suggested, by following the guiding principles of sustainable tourism, such as those proposed in the document *Tourism and the Environment: Maintaining the Balance* (ETB/DoE 1991) in the UK:

- The environment has an intrinsic value which outweighs its value as a tourism asset. Its enjoyment by future generations and its long-term survival must not be prejudiced by short-term considerations.
- Tourism should be recognised as a positive activity with the potential to benefit the community and the place as well as the visitor.
- The relationship between tourism and the environment must be managed so that the environment is sustainable in the long term. Tourism must not be allowed to damage the resource, prejudice its future employment or bring unacceptable impacts.
- Tourism activities and developments should respect the scale, nature and character of the place in which they are sited.
- In any location, harmony must be sought between the needs of the visitor, the place and the host community.
- In a dynamic world some change is inevitable and change can often be beneficial. Adaptation to change, however, should not be at the expense of any of these principles.
- The tourism industry, local authorities and environmental agencies all have a duty to respect the above principles and to work together to achieve their practical realisation.

In the context of rural tourism development, the principles of sustainable tourism are both logical and attractive, particularly when it is considered that, in many countries, not only is the countryside a repository of natural and built heritage (Lane 1994b), but also it is that heritage or rurality (see Chapter 1) that attracts many visitors to rural areas. Nevertheless, many commentators remain suspicious of the concept, questioning whether it is sustaining the tourism industry (i.e. continual development for economic gain) or sustaining the environment (i.e. no development for conservation) that is the prime objective (McKercher 1993). This tends to overlook the fact that sustainable rural tourism development is, ideally, a holistic process; its aim is to sustain the rural environment, the rural economy, the structure and culture of local rural communities, the experience of visitors and the long-term viability of the tourism industry in rural areas.

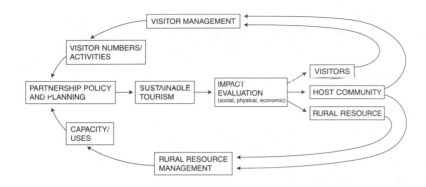

Figure 6.4 A conceptual model for the implementation of sustainable rural tourism
Source: adapted from Hvenegaard (1994)

However, there is still much debate as to whether the concept of sustainable rural tourism is achievable in practice and, if so, whether it is applicable to anything but small-scale, localised projects. Figure 6.4 illustrates a possible model for the implementation of sustainable rural tourism and, from this, it is evident that the success of a sustainable approach is dependent on a number of factors, including community involvement in planning, a partnership approach, and effective visitor management. Each of these is discussed briefly below.

COMMUNITY INVOLVEMENT IN RURAL TOURISM

A feature common to much of the literature on sustainable tourism is the assertion that a 'community-based approach to tourism development is a prerequisite to sustainability' (Woodley 1993). Underlying this is the belief that, frequently, the local community is a core component of the tourism destination or product and that 'healthy, thriving communities are the touchstone for a successful tourism industry' (Haywood 1988). Certainly, studies have shown that residents' attitudes towards tourism development can be both positive and negative (for example, see Ross 1992 for an analysis of resident perceptions of tourism impacts in Cairns, Australia, and Lankford 1994) and that, generally, increases in the scale and level of development of tourism are frequently mirrored by greater antagonism towards tourism amongst local people.

Thus, community-based tourism planning is seen to be necessary for two reasons. First, on a practical level, if the development of tourism is not compatible with a community's desires and objectives, when outside interests dominate local tourism or when residents' 'thresholds of tolerance for tourism and tourists are exceeded' (Haywood 1988), then conflicts and tensions are likely to occur which, ultimately, could result in the decline of tourism. Secondly, local residents, arguably, have the moral right to be involved in the development of an industry which is likely to result in both benefits and costs to their community. This is particularly so in the context of rural tourism where, frequently, local people have a 'symbiotic relationship' (Getz and Jamal 1994) with their environment. In other words, for many residents the rural environment is an essential ingredient of their quality of life and, therefore, any potential threat to that environment, such as the development of tourism, may be seen as a social cost.

Community involvement in tourism appears, therefore, to be a desirable and necessary element of sustainable tourism development, especially in the case of rural tourism. In fact, much of the early research into community-based planning (Murphy 1983; 1985) may be seen as laying the foundations for the current approach to sustainable tourism, its fundamental aim being to suggest ways in which 'the industry and its community base can benefit mutually from a long-term partnership' (Murphy 1983).

Since the 1980s, a number of attempts have been made to suggest ways in which local communities can play a more positive role in tourism planning although, as Woodley (1993) points out, examples of successfully applied community-based tourism schemes are relatively rare, perhaps as a result of many of the pitfalls inherent in the approach. It also, perhaps, not surprising that most community-based tourism development projects have occurred in rural areas. One of the larger-scale projects has been the Community Tourism Action Plan (CTAP) in Alberta, Canada, which was launched by Alberta Tourism, the provincial tourism authority, in 1987. Designed to help local communities to develop and implement their own tourism plans as a means of diversifying their economies, local volunteer Tourism Action Committees were encouraged to draw up and set in place their plans, backed up by a total of $30 million of state funding. By 1990, 54 per cent of the 429 eligible communities in Alberta had formally endorsed plans (Getz and Jamal 1994) whilst another 58 communities were in the process of preparing plans, but there has been wide variation in the success or viability of different schemes. Many small-scale community-based projects have been implemented throughout Europe (see Countryside Commission 1995b for an analysis of 21 projects in the UK) and in the United States the 'OuR-TOWN' (On-line Recreation and Tourism Opportunities Network) tourism project has been established to facilitate the development of sustainable tourism in rural communities.

To a great extent, most community-based tourism projects suffer from similar problems and barriers which limit their effectiveness. These include the domination of individual, short-term economic goals over longer term community objectives, the necessity for outside public or private sector finance which undermines local control, a lack of training, and a lack of interest, commitment or vision amongst those community members not directly involved in tourism (Woodley 1993; Countryside Commission 1995b). What has become evident is that, although some community input is vital for sustainable rural tourism development, it must be part of a broader, integrated strategy which involves a variety of public and private sector organisations within a recognised partnership.

PARTNERSHIPS IN RURAL TOURISM DEVELOPMENT

The planning and management of rural tourism potentially involves a large number of organisations, from both the public and private sectors, which are either directly or indirectly involved in tourism. Generally, public sector organisations are concerned with the provision of services, the formulation and implementation of rural development policies (including tourism) and resolving land-use conflicts; the private sector's main interest is financial gain. Sandwiched between the two, of course, lies the voluntary sector in the form of conservation bodies or pressure groups, many of which favour the 'no development' option. Therefore, it is inevitable that, sooner or later, the aims and objectives of the principal 'players' in the rural tourism system will come into conflict.

Implicitly, however, all organisations, including the tourism industry, share the same longer term objective, namely, the sustainable use of the countryside. However, whilst there is little disagreement about the *ends*, questions still remain about the *means* of achieving sustainable rural tourism and the debate has been focused, in particular, on the issue of control. On the one hand, many support the view that sustainable tourism can only be achieved by the 'top-down' approach, whereby a legal or regulatory framework is established which sets the environmental parameters within which the tourism industry is able to operate. Fundamental to this argument is the assumption that the multitude of organisations which comprise the tourism industry individually make decisions based on short-term profit motives.

On the other hand, there are those who advocate the 'bottom-up' approach, whereby the tourism industry is permitted to move towards sustainability through self-, rather than externally imposed, regulation. In other words, the onus is placed on the industry to formulate its own sustainable goals and working practices and to ensure that individual organisations, through measures such as industry codes of practice, work towards the common goal of sustainable development.

In practice, what is required is a balance between the 'top-down' and the 'bottom-up' approaches and it is generally accepted that 'constructive partnerships between industry, local populations and their representative governments are a necessary condition for sustainability' (Middleton 1996). In many countries, the regulatory and policy framework already exists in terms of environmental controls and rural development, frequently supported by national or regional funding schemes. At the same time, the tourism industry itself is recognising the importance of the sustainable use of the rural resource base and increasingly, rural tourism development schemes are being based upon the working partnerships between relevant public and private sector organisations (see Sharpley 1996: 246); Case study 10 briefly describes one such partnership.

Case study 11: The Tarka Project

The Tarka Project was established in 1989 as a means of integrating conservation, recreation and tourism in north Devon in England. The primary purpose of the project was to encourage the allocation of resources to conservation by demonstrating that conservation and tourism development can be mutually beneficial and that, together, they can contribute to the economic and social well-being of local communities.

The project was based on an extensive rural area of north Devon lying between the popular holiday resorts on the coast and the Dartmoor and Exmoor National Parks. Despite the popularity of the region as a whole as a tourist destination, it was felt that the project area itself lacked a clear identity and, indeed, it was attracting just 1 per cent of Devon's visitors. However, the area had been the setting of Henry Williamson's classic 1920s novel *Tarka the Otter* and, therefore, the Tarka theme was selected as the basis for the planned conservation and tourism initiatives.

The aims of the project were to:

● protect and enrich the wildlife, natural beauty and special character of north Devon;
● encourage public enjoyment and understanding of the area;
● promote tourism and recreation.

The running of the project was initially based upon a partnership between various organisations, both statutory and voluntary as well as local and national. These included local councils, the regional tourist board, the Countryside Commission and the Rural Development Commission. However, after three years, the Tarka Project launched the Tarka Country Tourist Association (TCTA) as a means of involving the private sector and it was not long before the membership of the Association, which then took over most of the marketing functions of the Tarka Project, stood at more than 150 private sector organisations.

There were three distinct phases to the project. Initially, efforts and resources were concentrated on conservation work and the development of the Tarka Trail, a 180 mile long distance walking route around the area serving as the focus for tourism development. A 30 mile stretch of the trail is also a popular cycle route attracting about 75,000 cyclists during the four month summer season. The second phase concentrated on developing industry support through the creation of the TCTA and other initiatives and, finally, the project was concerned with consolidating its achievements through effective marketing and interpretation.

It is generally accepted that the Tarka Project achieved its original aims and strong local supported resulted in funding for the project being extended to 1977. Although it is unclear to what extent visitor numbers have been increased during the life of the project, a clear identity for the area has been established and adopted by a variety of businesses, there is greater appreciation of the link between tourism and conservation, and the development of the partnership with the private sector means the work of the Tarka Project will be continued by the TCTA well beyond the 'life' of the project itself.

Source: Devon County Council (1988; 1993); Countryside Commission (1995b)

Inevitably, questions remain about the extent to which true, balanced partnerships can exist and, particularly, the extent to which the views of local communities are taken into consideration. Nevertheless, the partnership approach represents a positive planning and management process which, by taking broader social and environmental issues into account, goes some way towards achieving the objectives of sustainable tourism development. A final, yet important, consideration, is the vital contribution that visitor management also makes to the achievement of those objectives.

VISITOR MANAGEMENT

The idea that visitors to the countryside should be subject to some degree of control or influence appears, at first sight, to contradict the very meaning of rural tourism. As Jim (1989) argues, 'regulations are the antithesis of recreation, which connotes the spirit of freedom and spontaneity in the voluntary pursuit of pleasurable and rewarding experience in a preferred setting' and, as suggested in Chapter 3, many people are motivated to visit the countryside in order to escape from the restrictions and order of everyday, urban life.

Nevertheless, visitor management is a vital ingredient of the rural tourism management process. All visitors, knowingly or unknowingly, impact upon the rural environment (Sidaway 1988) and if a balance is to be achieved between the needs of local communities, the protection of the rural environment and the enjoyment of visitors, then management systems must be introduced to ensure that the behaviour of visitors is appropriate to the setting. In other words, sustainable rural tourism is, in effect, a function of both sustainable planning and development and sustainable tourist activities; usually, the latter can only be achieved through effective visitor management.

Visitor management encompasses a range of measures that may be introduced by tourism planners and managers to directly or indirectly influence the activities of visitors in rural areas. In other words, it is concerned with exerting some control over where tourists go in the countryside, and what they do when they get there. However, it is important that visitor management schemes are unobtrusive. That is, they should be implemented in such a way that the sense of freedom and spontaneity that is synonymous with rural tourism is maintained as far as possible whilst minimising the adverse impacts of visitors' activities. Therefore, visitor management schemes should, ideally, strive to *influence*, rather than *regulate*, visitor behaviour and one popular method of achieving this is through codes of conduct. For example, many sports organisations publish codes of conduct for their members whilst, more generally, tourist brochures often suggest appropriate behaviour at tourist sites. The code of conduct in Figure 6.5 refers to the 'Canyon Country' of South Eastern Utah in the United States, an area which includes Canyonlands and Arches National Parks and a number of state parks.

Codes of conduct are, essentially, non-enforceable guidelines and, therefore, the extent to which they are complied with depends upon the willingness of visitors to modify their behaviour and to accept their responsibility to the environment. Thus, in many cases, more regulatory forms of visitor management may be required to control and manage visitors. A complete discussion of all visitor management techniques is not possible here (see Sharpley 1996), but a variety of methods may be used to influence, redistribute and, where necessary, restrict tourism in the countryside, including marketing programmes, traffic management and, most commonly, zoning schemes (Murphy 1985: 62). However, the important point here is that visitor management is not separate from, but part of, the rural tourism planning and management process. Rural tourism cannot be sustainable unless the activities of tourists themselves are sustainable and, as the demands and pressures on rural areas become more intense and new forms of recreational activities become popular, it is likely that the need for effective visitor management will become increasingly urgent.

**Canyon Country
Minimum Impact Practices**

1.   Tread lightly when travelling and leave no trace of your camping
Drive and ride only on roads and trails where such travel is allowed, established trails, on rocks, or in washes. Camp at designated sites or, where allowed, at previously used sites. Avoid placing tents on top of vegetation and use a camp stove instead of making a camp fire. Unless signs indicate otherwise, leave gates open or closed as you find them.

2.   Help keep Canyon Country clean.
Pack out your trash and recycle it, clean up after less thoughtful visitors, and dispose of human waste properly

3.   Protect and conserve scarce desert water resources.
Camp at least 300 feet from isolated water sources to allow for wildlife access. Where possible, carry your own drinking water. Leave potholes undisturbed and wash well away from pools and springs.

4.   Allow space for wildlife
When encountering wildlife, maintain your distance and remain quiet. Teach children not to chase or pick up animals. Keep pets under control.

5.   Leave historic sites, Native American rock art, ruins and artefacts untouched for the future.
Admire rock art from a distance and never touch it. Stay out of ruins, leave artefacts in place, and report violations.

Source: South-eastern Utah Travel Guide (n.d.)

Figure 6.5 Behavioural code for visitors to Canyon Country

CONCLUSION

There is no doubt that tourism can play an important role in the regeneration and diversification of rural economies and communities. At the same time, tourism can also act as a catalyst for the protection and renovation of rural environments and, therefore, it is not surprising that, in many countries, tourism is viewed as a panacea to the ills suffered by rural areas.

However, as has been suggested in this chapter, effective planning and management is necessary to ensure that the benefits of tourism development are optimised whilst the costs, or negative impacts, on the host environment and community are minimised. This requires an approach to planning that is both integrated and holistic, ensuring that tourism is a means of achieving the balanced and sustainable development of rural areas rather than an end in itself. Therefore, community involvement, partnerships between all the relevant individuals and organisations and effective visitor management schemes are all integral elements of the planning and management process.

Furthermore, it is a process which should be continual. New or increasing demands and pressures are placed on rural areas and new recreational activities emerge, yet the countryside is finite and fragile. Therefore, innovative approaches to planning and managing the rural resource base for tourism are required and new issues and problems must be faced. It is with some of these issues that the final chapter is concerned.

QUESTIONS

1. What are the potential benefits of effective planning and management of rural tourism?
2. Describe and justify the typical stages of the rural tourism planning process.
3. To what extent is community involvement an essential prerequisite for the development of sustainable tourism?
4. Why is visitor management necessary in the context of rural tourism?

FURTHER READING

Bramwell, B. and Lane, B. (1994) *Rural Tourism and Sustainable Rural Development*, Bristol: Channel View Publications.

Croall, J. (1995) *Preserve or Destroy: Tourism and the Environment*, London: Calouste Gulbenkian Foundation.

ETB (1991) *Tourism and the Environment: Maintaining the Balance*, London: English Tourist Board.

Gunn, C. (1994) *Tourism Planning: Basics, Concepts, Cases,* 3rd edition, London: Taylor and Francis.

Murphy, P. (1985) *Tourism: A Community Approach*, London: Routledge.

Nelson, J., Butler, R. and Wall, G. (eds) (1993) *Tourism and Sustainable Development: Monitoring, Planning, Managing*, University of Waterloo: Department of Geography.

7 Issues in rural tourism

INTRODUCTION

This book is intended as a broad introduction to the study of rural tourism and, inevitably, many important topics and issues are not considered in as much detail as they perhaps deserve. For example, the role of national parks as a means of balancing the demands of tourism and conservation, the planning of sustainable rural tourism development, specific marketing techniques, or methods of managing tourists in the countryside are each of fundamental importance to the study of rural tourism, yet space does not permit a more in-depth analysis of these subjects.

However, throughout the book a number of key themes have emerged:

- Tourism is being increasingly viewed and promoted as an effective vehicle for the economic and socio-cultural regeneration and diversification of rural areas.
- The demand for rural tourism is likely to grow as second holidays, short breaks and alternatives to the traditional package-type holiday become increasingly popular.
- To most visitors, the appeal of the countryside is the sense of space, freedom, tranquillity, traditional 'rurality' and the opportunities for spontaneous and informal recreational activities.
- The development of rural tourism must be carefully planned and managed so that tourism does not degrade or damage the resource upon which it depends.

In short, there are likely to be, on the one hand, ever increasing demands placed on the countryside as a resource for tourism, both from those who wish to visit and enjoy the particular qualities and characteristics of rural areas and from those who try to exploit the countryside for commercial reasons, and, on the other hand, greater calls for the protection and conservation of the countryside. In the latter case, it will not only be the more traditional pressure groups and conservation agencies that will be lobbying for an increase in protective measures within rural planning and management; both visitors and rural residents, in particular those who are more recent members of rural communities, will be striving to protect 'their' countryside from what they consider to be damaging or inappropriate development.

In order to maintain the balance between these potentially conflicting demands on the countryside, a number of important issues will need to be taken into consideration by those with responsibility for the planning and management of rural tourism. In particular, the demand for greater access to and within rural areas needs to be addressed and means of integrating this demand within the sustainable use of the countryside must be found. At the same time, other concerns, such as the effects of second-home ownership and the socio-cultural impacts of counter-urbanisation, are also of increasing relevance. It is these issues that are the focus of this concluding chapter.

ACCESS ISSUES

Rural tourism is, simply, about people. It is about tourists who visit and enjoy the countryside and who, in order to do so, must be able to travel to and within rural areas. In other words, for rural tourism to exist and, by implication, for it to benefit local communities, people must have *access* to the countryside. As tourism is increasingly developed in rural areas and as the demand for rural tourism grows, so too will there be a greater need for access. However, that access needs to be balanced not only with all the other demands on the countryside but also with the longer term protection or conservation of the rural resource. As more tourists demand access and as rural planners and managers, eager to jump on the rural tourism bandwagon, supply more opportunities for access, the greater will be the pressures placed on the countryside by tourists and the tourism industry. For example, even in Sweden it has been suggested that *allemansrätt,* the traditional free right of access to the countryside (see Chapter 4), should be limited to Swedish citizens as a result of concern over the misuse of these rights by overseas tourists (Sandell 1995).

Thus, a challenge inherent in the development and management of rural tourism is how to balance access with the protection of the rural environment. Indeed, in many countries it is now one of the most pressing issues as various groups, such as the Ramblers Association in the UK, call for greater access, as newer forms of recreational activities, such as mountain-biking or off-highway 4-wheel driving, become more widespread, and as the conservation lobby becomes more powerful. Within this context, two particular issues have attracted increasing attention and debate: first, it has been suggested that people should be required to pay to visit the countryside and, second, there have been increasing calls for the introduction of more sustainable forms of transport.

WHAT PRICE THE COUNTRYSIDE?

The idea that people should pay to visit the countryside or, more accurately, pay entry fees to specific sites, facilities or attractions within the rural setting, is by no means new. For example, in the United States 'the first federal recreation fees were auto-entry permits collected at Mount Rainer National Park in 1908' (Harris and Driver 1987) and, by 1916, the entry fee there was $6 per vehicle whilst Yosemite and Yellowstone National Parks were charging $8 and $10 respectively (Walsh 1986). Nowadays, most national parks in the United States charge for entrance, as do many state parks and other recreational sites, and visits to national parks, nature reserves and other designated areas in many other countries around the world are also subject to entry fees. Similarly, tourists have long been required to pay for the use of certain rural tourism facilities, such as campsites, or for entry to rural attractions, such as museums, country houses and historic or archaeological sites. Importantly, in most of the above cases, the fees collected contribute towards the management costs of the park or attraction, or go towards the costs of providing tourist facilities, such as toilets, information services or picnic areas.

However, as concern for the environmental impacts of rural tourism has grown, increasing attention has been focused on the potential role of access fees as a means of reducing some of the pressures and tourism-related problems in rural areas. In other words, as the demand for rural tourism has grown and the carrying capacity of many popular destination areas has been exceeded, resulting in unsustainable levels of recreational use and, in some cases, serious damage to the physical fabric of the countryside, it has been argued that putting a price on rural recreation could be an effective means of alleviating some of these problems. In short, it has been suggested that people should, generally, pay to visit the countryside.

Inevitably, such a proposal does not attract universal support and many argue that charging for access to the countryside would be neither practical nor ethical. In particular, rural recreation in general is widely considered to be good for both the individual and for society as a whole (in other words, a 'merit' good) and should, therefore, 'be promoted and provided free of direct user charge' (McCallum and Adams 1980). At the same time, free and wide access to the countryside is also seen as a moral right and charging would, therefore, represent an infringement or restriction on personal freedom. Nevertheless, there is an increasing body of literature concerned with the issue of charging for rural recreation (for example, see Cullen 1985; Hanley 1989; Stokes 1989; Sharpley 1993) within which charging for access to the countryside is considered from two main perspectives: pricing as a visitor management tool and pricing as a means of supporting conservation.

Access charges: pricing for visitor management

Bovaird *et al.* (1984) suggest that the demand for rural tourism is influenced by four factors, namely accessibility, 'affordability', the weather and personal preferences. Given the spontaneous nature of much rural tourism, the weather plays a significant role in demand, whilst distance and the availability of transport (accessibility) and personal motivations as outlined in Chapter 3 are normally considered prime influences on the level of demand. However, affordability (ability to pay) and preferences (willingness to pay) are also seen as factors which affect the demand for rural tourism and by implication, therefore, pricing can be used to manipulate, or ration, demand.

The use of pricing for visitor management is based on the idea that rural tourism is an economic activity and that tourists, as 'consumers' of the rural tourism product, place a value on visiting the countryside. Therefore, if a visit to the countryside is 'free' then, in theory, all those people who wish to participate in rural tourism will do so. However, different people inevitably place different values on rural tourism, both as a distinct activity and also in relation to other forms of tourism. As a result, if the cost of a trip to the countryside increases, only those people who place a higher value on rural tourism compared with other activities will continue to visit the countryside, as long as the expected benefits remain greater than the costs of a visit. In short, 'rationing by price guarantees that those who most avidly desire wilderness access, as measured by willingness to pay, will obtain it' (Fractor 1982).

Similarly, pricing can, in theory, be used as a visitor management tool at specific sites within the countryside to ration demand. If charges are introduced at certain popular or over-used areas then a proportion of visitors are likely to be influenced to go to alternative, free destinations in the countryside. In New Zealand, for example, one study found that of six different rationing devices utilised as a means of controlling and allocating the recreational use of public land, pricing appeared to be the best in terms of efficiency and equity (Cullen 1985). However, other studies in the United States have shown that, in practice, the effect of charging on the demand for countryside recreation can, in the longer term, actually result in an *increase* in demand (Walsh 1986) and that, if the introduction of pricing is publicised as a contribution to conservation, then it is strongly supported by visitors (Leuschner *et al.* 1987). Thus, the introduction of pricing is unlikely to have a significant impact as a means of controlling the demand for access to the countryside and, therefore, it is of more relevance in terms of the contribution it can make to rural conservation.

Access charges: pricing for conservation

Implicit in the arguments that rural recreation is a merit good and that the citizens of a country have a moral right of free access to 'their' land is the belief that the recreational use of the countryside should be subsidised by the state and, therefore, that it should be the state that 'picks up the tab' for the cost of any repair work or conservation resulting from tourism-induced impacts. In other words, from the point of view of both tourists and the tourism industry, the countryside is seen as a free resource, a perspective which is supported by the findings of one survey in the UK which found that 75 per cent of tourism businesses in or bordering national parks made no contribution to conservation projects in the parks.

However, in environmental economics terms, such an approach is unsustainable. For any economic activity, including tourism, to be sustainable in the long term and for scarce resources to be allocated and used rationally, the full cost of that activity must be 'internalised' by the producer and, inevitably, passed onto the consumer. In other words, the cost of producing any good or service should include environmental costs, such as the costs of pollution control, and the price paid by the consumer should reflect those costs. This is the basic tenet of what is known as the Polluter Pays Principle, which forms the basis for many environmental policies throughout the world.

It is not possible here, of course, to consider environmental economics and the Polluter Pays Principle in detail, although useful introductions can be found in Pearce *et al.* (1989), Norton (1992) or Turner (1993). However, if the principles of environmental economics are applied to rural tourism, it can be argued that both the rural tourism industry and countryside visitors themselves should be responsible for the environmental costs resulting from tourism development. That is, for rural tourism to be sustainable, the costs of repairing and conserving the countryside as the basic resource that supports tourism should be met by those who benefit from it. For example, it has been estimated that the total cost of repairing the damaged and eroded paths along the more fragile sections of the Pennine Way, the UK's longest and most popular National Trail, will amount to over £5 million. These costs are currently met by various public organisations but some might argue that it would be justifiable to charge people to walk along the trail, thereby contributing to both repair costs and to the enjoyment of future generations of walkers.

Access charges: issues and problems

There are, inevitably, a number of issues and problems inherent in the concept of charging for access to the wider countryside (as opposed to charging for access to specific managed rural tourism sites and attractions where, in many cases, entry fees already exist). As mentioned earlier, many consider access to the countryside to be a moral right and the introduction of entry fees or user fees would, therefore, be seen as an infringement of personal liberties. Furthermore, most domestic tourists in the countryside already pay for access, albeit indirectly, through tax payments, subsidies and voluntary donations to relevant organisations. Thus, access charges could be seen as an unjustifiable and additional financial burden on visitors.

Another frequent argument against charging for access is that it would ration demand by ability to pay and would, therefore, be elitist. However, most other forms of tourism are, in effect, rationed by price and rural tourism itself, usually involving transport costs, refreshments and so on, is not 'free'. Moreover, the socio-economic profile of the majority of rural tourists suggests that those who would be potentially discriminated against tend not to visit the countryside and research in the United States has demonstrated that 'the imposition of . . . user fees would not tend to discriminate against the poor' (Vaux 1975).

The greatest problems, however, would be of a practical nature, in terms of who, when, where, how and how much to charge. There is, for example, little agreement as to how to place an economic value on a visit to the countryside, with three different methods (travel-cost method, contingent valuation method and hedonic pricing method) currently being utilised. Other problems to be addressed include how to collect entry fees, with options ranging from voluntary donation points ('honesty boxes') or permits to manned collection points, who to charge (should local people be excluded?) and when (all year or seasonally?). Together, these questions suggest that charging for access to the countryside is unlikely to be a viable proposition in the near future although one effective means of collecting contributions is through the imposition of a bed tax, a system which already operates in some European countries. Generally, however, it is recognised that all forms of tourism, including rural tourism, to be sustainable, they will, in the future, have to pay their way.

SUSTAINABLE TRANSPORT IN THE COUNTRYSIDE

One of the most pressing and, perhaps, emotive issues in the planning and development of rural tourism, particularly in the industrialised world, is the role of the motor car as a means of travelling to, and around, the countryside. Indeed, concern for the impacts of transport in general, and the car in particular, is central to environmental studies and the challenge of sustainable development as transport has been identified as one of the key factors in the accelerating deterioration of global environmental quality (Whitelegg 1993).

Much of the attention is focused on the contribution of transport to air pollution and global warming, and figures describing exhaust emissions and pollution are frequently cited to emphasise the environmental impacts of different modes of transport. For example, it has been found that, in the UK, vehicle emissions account for over 17 per cent of carbon dioxide, 45 per cent of nitrogen oxides and 85 per cent of carbon monoxide (Transport 2000 1989). As carbon dioxide alone contributes about 50 per cent of the global warming effect, the impact of road transport on that phenomenon is, therefore, significant, and likely to become more so. On a national basis, road traffic in the UK, in terms of vehicle miles, is forecast to rise by between 83 per cent and 142 per cent by 2025, but globally, just 8 per cent of the world's population owns a car; the potential growth in worldwide car ownership and, hence in environmental impacts, is enormous.

In the context of rural tourism, however, it is not only the atmospheric pollution effects of the car that are of concern. Again in the UK, some 57 per cent of all motorised traffic is on rural roads and motorways, although only 11 per cent of the population lives outside urban areas, and it has been suggested that rural traffic might grow by between 127 per cent and 267 per cent by 2025 (Countryside Commission 1992). This growth is likely to lead to increased congestion, particularly at peak holiday periods, resulting in greater inconvenience for both local communities and visitors, but it will also exacerbate a number of other environmental and social problems associated with the use of the car in rural areas. In particular:

- Increasing car ownership and usage has led to a decline in public transport services in many rural areas. Not only does this reduce the mobility of rural residents who do not own, or do not wish to use, a car, but it also reduces the accessibility of the countryside for potential tourists who do not have the use of a car.
- Air pollution from traffic may have longer term impacts on the flora and fauna in rural areas and, in Europe, it is recognised that extensive tracts of woodland in Germany and Scandinavia have been damaged by car emissions and 'acid rain'.
- Congestion and major traffic flows cause both visual and noise pollution. Long queues of slow moving or stationary traffic visually intrude on the scenic quality of the countryside whilst excessive noise levels can also disturb the peace of the rural environment.
- In response to increasing car ownership and usage, the transport policy of many countries has been to build more roads, or to improve and widen existing roads, to accommodate greater levels of traffic. In many areas, this has given rise to serious concern over the loss of natural habitats, the destruction of important natural or historical sites and, more generally, the paving over of rural areas.
- Road building leads to the development of 'by-products', such as car parks, lay-bys, roadside restaurants, petrol stations and other facilities designed to serve the car-bound tourist. These may also result in indirect impacts on the countryside. For example, car parks tend to concentrate visitors at particular sites, thereby causing greater erosion on nearby footpaths.

This list is by no means exhaustive and, of course, not all rural areas suffer the same variety or level of impacts. Much depends on the physical characteristics and fragility of different areas, the level of recreational use, population densities, the availability of rural areas and so on and in countries such as the UK or Holland (the latter being the most densely populated in Europe), the issue of sustainable transport is likely to be much higher on the environmental agenda than in countries such as the United States or Canada. Nevertheless, road transport and specifically the motor car is, more generally, considered to be the least sustainable form of transport in terms of its impact on the environment and society. That is, although for the individual traveller the car is one of the cheapest and most convenient and flexible forms of motorised transport, its costs to society in terms of energy use, pollution, land use and health care are virtually incalculable (see Pearce 1993). Moreover, with reference to rural tourism in particular, it is widely accepted that, although the car is the most popular means of transport for travelling to and around the countryside, it represents one of the greatest threats to the physical and socio-cultural well-being of rural areas, particularly in the more popular rural tourism destinations. It is not surprising, therefore, that alternative and more sustainable forms of transport are being sought by rural tourism planners and managers.

Solutions to the traffic problem

It has been suggested (Mitchell 1991) there are four possible solutions to the problems associated with the use of the motor car in rural areas:

To allow congestion to act as its own deterrent

The simplest approach may be to allow the countryside to become so busy that people no longer wish to visit it. However, congestion is, frequently, localised and seasonal, most car drivers are becoming used to traffic jams – it is estimated that Americans spend around two billion man-hours each year sitting in traffic jams (Whitelegg 1993) – and would, in fact, result in greater environmental impacts.

To improve the road network and car park provision

Whilst building new roads, improving existing ones and providing more car parking improves accessibility in the short term, it is now accepted that, in the longer term, the net effect is simply to increase the overall amount of traffic. Therefore, in many rural areas, such as the national parks in the UK, the policy is now to implement traffic management schemes that match the level of traffic to the existing road network rather than adapting roads to accommodate greater volumes of traffic.

To restrict or regulate car access

The restriction or regulation of car access is common in many urban areas and it is an obvious solution to the problems facing popular rural tourist destinations. A number of experimental schemes have been successfully implemented in the UK, such as in the Derwent Valley in the Peak District National Park, where roads are closed to motorised traffic and visitors are encouraged to explore the region on bicycles. More permanently, the use of private cars is now banned in Yosemite National Park in the United States and visitors are required to use the provided transport system. However, such schemes are only viable in managed areas where access may be restricted.

To develop and promote effective public transport

An efficient, cheap and integrated public transport system is considered by many to be the only realistic means of overcoming the problems of transport to and within the countryside. Indeed, it is generally seen as the only *sustainable* form of transport and there are undoubted social and environmental benefits associated with it. For example, an effective public transport system improves the accessibility of rural areas, it significantly reduces the environmental impacts that result from widespread car usage, particularly when travel by rail is compared with road travel, it is more healthy when linked in to local forms of sustainable transport such as cycling, and it has the potential to improve the rural tourism experience by allowing people to enjoy the scenery without the responsibility of driving.

However, experience has shown that the successful implementation of public transport faces a number of hurdles. Importantly, public transport, particularly in rural areas where demand may be related to the tourism seasons, tends to be unprofitable and, therefore, operators require a significant level of financial subsidy which, certainly in most Western economies, is no longer forthcoming. Services must also be integrated at both the local and national level in order to make public transport easy to use, information and timetables need to be easily and widely available, and it must be effectively promoted because 'any recreational [public] transport scheme is only as good as its marketing' (Countryside Commission 1987c). Perhaps the greatest hurdle, however, is the attitude of car owners. No other form of transport can match the flexibility, privacy and comfort of the car and it has become, in effect, 'a detachable extension of the home' (Bannister 1988). Many societies have now become car dependent and broader development policies relating, for example, to housing, recreation and shopping are based around private car ownership and usage. Therefore, significant inducements would be required to encourage people to leave their cars at home.

Tourism is, of course, synonymous with transport and, to participate in rural tourism, visitors must be able to travel to and around the countryside. Moreover, a major attraction of rural tourism is the opportunity to do so spontaneously and freely. However, the car, as a symbol of that freedom and spontaneity, also poses a major threat to the attraction of rural areas and, therefore, what is perhaps required is a combination of greater investment in public transport, restrictions on car access, taxation and pricing policies, a shift in national transport policies and effective marketing and public awareness programmes. In some areas, a more proactive approach to the rural transport problem has been attempted; in the UK, for example, the Lake District Traffic Management Initiative was a project that combined the development of a roads hierarchy based on community and visitor needs with public transport and effective marketing. However, as an indication of the inherent problems of such schemes, the proposals were shelved indefinitely in 1996 as a result of public opposition yet, until similar projects and schemes become more widespread and gain public support, the use of the car in the countryside will, arguably, remain the greatest obstacle to development of sustainable rural tourism.

HOUSING ISSUES IN THE COUNTRYSIDE

It has long been recognised that one of the major infrastructural changes brought about by the growth of tourism in rural areas has been the increased level of second home ownership, particularly in the more popular destination areas (see Coppock 1977; Mathieson and Wall 1982: 126). For example, in the English Lake District as a whole about 16 per cent of all properties are second or holiday homes whilst in some specific parts of the region over one third of properties fall into this category. Similarly, in the county of Norfolk up to 11 per cent of houses are unoccupied by permanent residents (ACORA 1990), reflecting a pattern of property ownership and use found in many other rural areas.

Given these high levels of second home ownership it is not, perhaps, surprising that many of the housing-related problems facing rural communities are blamed upon tourism. Indeed, in extreme cases action may be taken against second home owners, as occurred in North Wales during the 1980s when a number of properties were fire-bombed in protest at the number of holiday homes owned by English people. Such reactions are rare but, as discussed shortly, there are nevertheless a number of problems that may be attributed to tourism-induced home ownership in rural areas. At the same time, however, it is important to point out that other changes are occurring in the pattern and structure of rural property ownership, resulting in particular from the process of counter-urbanisation, which may also have significant impacts on rural society and, perhaps, on the potential for tourism development in rural areas.

Second home ownership

To blame all the problems associated with housing in rural areas on second home ownership is to ignore a number of broader related issues, such as planning policies, restrictions on housing development and building schemes, and trends and changes in the market for rented property. However, it is generally accepted that, beyond minimum levels, the outside ownership (and temporary use) of second or holiday homes has a number of impacts on rural communities. In some cases, these impacts may be beneficial. For example, old or redundant buildings may be renovated or converted into housing, thus improving the visual quality of an area, local people may be employed on a temporary or permanent basis by the owners of second homes and extra spending in local shops and other facilities will be generated.

More commonly, extensive second home ownership in rural areas is associated with a number of negative impacts. In terms of physical impacts, Mathieson and Wall (1982: 126) argue that new developments can seriously degrade the landscape, both visually and through vegetation clearance, suggesting that 'there has been little concern for aesthetically harmonious designs evident in most second home developments' (Mathieson and Wall 1982: 127). However, it is the social impacts of second home ownership that tend to be of greater concern. In particular:

- Extensive second home ownership significantly reduces the availability of housing for local people, particularly where planning policies restrict new home developments.
- The demand for second homes in popular rural areas raises the cost of housing to the extent that local people are no longer able to afford to buy houses. In the English national parks, for example, the cost of houses can be as much as 25 per cent above the national average.
- Younger people, unable to afford to live locally, move away to urban areas, disrupting the social structure of rural communities.
- The influx of wealthier 'outsiders' can lead to resentment within the local community and to a dilution of local culture, although studies have shown that second home owners do make efforts to integrate with local communities (for example, see Buller and Hoggart 1994 for a discussion of the social integration of British home owners in France).

Therefore, the challenge facing rural planners is the need to find a balance between the demands of wealthier urban residents wishing to buy holiday residences in the countryside and the housing requirements of local communities. Often, the answer is seen to lie in low-cost housing schemes for local residents, where new homes are made available for rent or purchase at realistic rates. However, wider issues, such as employment opportunities and the provision of services, such as health and education, are also part of the equation, whilst the situation is also further complicated by the process of counter-urbanisation now being experienced by many rural areas.

Counter-urbanisation

Counter-urbanisation is the term used to describe a reversal in the trend of rural–urban migration that has been experienced by many rural areas since the early 1800s. In other words, rural communities are now beginning to experience in-migration from urban areas and an overall increase in population levels. For example, in England the greatest population increases in recent years have been experienced by rural counties whilst the metropolitan areas have experienced a net loss in population (HMSO 1996).

There are a number of factors underlying this trend and, since the 1970s, when it was first identified (Champion and Watkins 1991), research has been increasingly undertaken into the reasons for and characteristics of counter-urbanisation, both nationally and internationally (see, for example, Champion 1989; Dean *et al.* 1984; Jones *et al.* 1986; Perry *et al.* 1986). It has been questioned, for example, whether it is simply the result of the outward spread of urbanisation from the metropolitan centres into rural areas or evidence of a more fundamental shift in social values in a post-industrial or post-modern era (Newby 1986; Murdoch and Pratt 1993). It is not possible here to examine these issues in detail but, generally, four reasons are evident for the phenomenon of counter-urbanisation (Bolton and Chalkey 1990):

- there is an increasing preference among people to live in rural, as opposed to urban areas, a theory supported by surveys into housing preferences;
- many businesses have relocated into rural areas to take advantage of lower costs, ease of transport and so on;
- state policies have favoured the redevelopment of and investment in rural areas, thus pulling jobs and people into previously declining areas;
- there have been wider economic and technological changes, both nationally and internationally, that have resulted in industrial re-structuring.

Of these, the most popular explanation tends to be that people simply wish to live in a rural environment for all the benefits, real and imagined (Newby 1985; Sinclair 1990) that might be gained. In this context, one of the major issues is the extent to which these rural newcomers integrate into the existing society and culture. It has been suggested, for example, that many of the new, ex-urban inhabitants of rural towns and villages bring with them 'a set of values said to emerge from rural communities of the past' (Cloke *et al.* 1991: 39). In so doing, they attempt to conserve a rural idyll whilst opposing any form of modern development that is likely to spoil their new-found rural lifestyle and, as Gammon (1996) argues, it has become 'almost as important to *live out* a type of romanticised home life than to *live in* a particular village community'. One result of this is that rural villages are in danger of becoming fossilised and prettified by their wealthier new inhabitants (Gammon 1996) and, in the context of rural tourism, the implications are contradictory. On the one hand, 'typical' rural villages will attract visitors eager to experience the image of rurality created, directly or indirectly, by counter-urbanisation but, on the other hand, tourists are unlikely to be welcomed by rural newcomers.

Whilst this is undoubtedly an extreme case, there is no doubt that rural areas and societies are more generally becoming subject to urban values, partly as a result of counter-urbanisation and partly as a result of broader structural changes in the countryside which have dramatically reduced the distinction between 'urban' and 'rural'. Agriculture is no longer dominant as new industries are located in rural areas, improved transport links have brought all but the most peripheral communities 'closer' to urban centres, population structures are changing and the demands of conservation (a concept firmly rooted in urban society) has come to dominate much rural planning. In short 'change is in the air and ... the challenge is to use any changes imaginatively' (Countryside Commission 1989b: 8). The ways in which rural tourism can be integrated into this changing rural environment is one of these challenges.

OTHER ISSUES AND FUTURE RESEARCH NEEDS

The issues discussed so far in this chapter are, perhaps, the most pressing and visible, but they are by no means the only ones relevant to the planning and management of rural tourism. Not only is the rural environment in a constant state of change and development but the demands placed upon it by society, and society itself, are also continually changing. Thus, new issues will continue to emerge and new research needs will present themselves.

In the context of access to the countryside there are two further issues with which, it is suggested, rural tourism planners should be concerned. First, there is a need for greater consideration to be given to providing rural recreational opportunities for disabled people. The access debate usually centres on issues such as citizens rights, the freedom to roam and legal rights of access (see Shoard 1996; Curry 1996; Ravenscroft 1996) but the needs of specific groups are frequently overlooked. In other words attention should not only be focused on maintaining or improving the right of access to the countryside but also the extent to which all people are able to exercise that right. In some areas, facilities, such as specially surfaced paths or gates suitable for wheelchair users, have been provided but, more generally, research needs to be undertaken into how best to provide access for disabled people, in particular to the wider, open countryside.

A second important access issue requiring further research is in relation to ethnic minority access to the countryside (see Kinsman 1996). As discussed in Chapter 3, participation in rural tourism is, by and large, socially defined. That is, those most likely to visit the countryside tend to be younger, professional, middle class people whilst, conversely, ethnic minorities are amongst those groups identified as experiencing difficulty in gaining access to the countryside (Countryside Commission 1991b). The reasons for this under-representation of ethnic minority groups in rural tourism are unclear. It may be that, on the one hand, minority groups do not share the same attachment to the countryside as the European middle classes; on the other hand, the countryside may be perceived as a threatening or unwelcoming landscape. Whatever the underlying causes, it has already been recognised by the Countryside Commission in England that there is a need to improve access opportunities for ethnic minority groups through, for example, improved countryside staff training, increased representation of minorities amongst countryside staff and the provision of relevant information and literature. Nevertheless, further research into this issue may reveal the needs and concerns of ethnic minority groups with respect to rural tourism and may also suggest means of achieving equality of access opportunities.

There are, of course, many other research issues directly and indirectly related to rural tourism, such as the role of tourism as a developmental tool in rural areas, the changing meaning of rurality and its link to the demand for rural, environmental impact assessment linked to the development of rural tourism, and so on. Indeed, as a multidisciplinary subject, the scope for research into rural tourism is enormous, whether from a geographical, environmental, marketing, economic, management, planning, political or sociological perspective. Each of these disciplines has much to offer to the study and understanding of rural tourism and many sections in this book have drawn on the literature from some, if not all, of them. At the same time, none of these disciplines can individually lay claim to the study of rural tourism and it is hoped that, in the future, the study of rural tourism will be increasingly recognised as a subject in its own right.

QUESTIONS

1. In the context of sustainable rural tourism, assess the advantages and problems of charging for access to the countryside.
2. How important are appropriate transport policies to the planning and management of rural tourism?
3. What are the implications of counter-urbanisation for the future development of rural tourism?
4. What are the contributions of different academic disciplines to the study of rural tourism?

FURTHER READING

Bishop, K. and Phillips, A. (1993) 'Seven Steps to Market – the Development of the Market-led Approach to Countryside Conservation and Recreation', *Journal of Rural Studies*, 9(4), 315–38.

Champion, T. and Watkins, C. (eds) (1991) *People in the Countryside*, London: PCP.

CRN (1995) *A Drive in the Country?: Examining the Problems of Recreational Travel and Working Towards Solutions*, Cardiff: Countryside Recreation Network.

Page, S. (1994) *Transport for Tourism*, London: Routledge.

Sinclair, D. (1990) *Shades of Green: Myth and Muddle in the Countryside*, London: Paladin.

Whitelegg, J. (1993) *Transport for a Sustainable Future: The Case for Europe*, London: Bellhaven Press.

References

ACORA (1990) *Faith in the Countryside*, Report of the Archbishops' Commission on Rural Areas, Worthing: Churchman Publishing.

Adler, J. (1989) 'Origins of Sightseeing', *Annals of Tourism Research* 16, 1: 7–29.

ADT (1994) *National Rural Tourism Strategy*, Australian Department of Tourism, Canberra: Australian Government Publishing Service.

Albert-Piñole, I. (1993) 'Tourism in Spain', in W. Pompll and P. Lavery (eds) *Tourism in Europe: Structures and Developments*, Wallingford: CAB International: 242–261.

Albright, H. and Cahn, R. (1985) *The Birth of the National Park Service*, Salt Lake City, Utah: Howe Brothers.

Andronikou, A. (1987) *Development of Tourism in Cyprus – Harmonisation of Tourism with the Environment*, Nicosia: Cyprus Tourism Organisation.

Ashworth, G. and Voogt, H. (1990) 'Can Places Be Sold For Tourism?', in G. Ashworth and B. Goodall (eds) *Marketing Tourism Places*, London: Routledge: 1–22.

Aslet, C. (1991) *Countryblast*, London: John Murray.

Australia Tourist Commission (1995) *National Parks – Fact Sheet*, London: Australia Tourist Commission.

Baker, M. (1991) *The Marketing Book,* 2nd edition, Oxford: Butterworth Heinemann.

Baldock, D. and Beaufoy, G. (1993) *Nature Conservation and New Directions in the EC Common Agricultural Policy*, Institute for European Environmental Policy.

Balogh, O. and Csaky, C. (1991) 'The Development of Rural Tourism in Hungary', *Tourism Recreation Research* **16**, 1: 25–28.

Bannister, D. (1988) 'Congestion and Gridlock in Britain', *Built Environment* 15, 3/4.

Baranowska-Janota, M. (1994) *Towards Sustainable Tourism in Polish National Parks*, Proceedings of Sustainable Tourism for the 21st Century Conference, Lagos, Portugal.

Barke, M. and Newton, M. (1994) 'A New Rural Development Initiative in Spain: the European Community's 'Plan LEADER''', *Geography* 79: 366–371.

Barke, M. and Newton, M. (1995) 'The EU LEADER Initiative and Rural Tourism Development: Applications in Spain', in N. Evans and

M. Robinson (eds) *Issues in Travel and Tourism Volume 1*, Sunderland: Business Education Publishers: 1–40.

de Beers, G. (1949) *Travellers in Switzerland*, Oxford: OUP.

Beioley, S. (1995) 'Green Tourism – Soft or Sustainable?', *ETB Insights*, London: English Tourist Board, B79–89.

Berry, G. and Beard, G. (1980) *The Lake District: A Century of Conservation*, Edinburgh: John Bartholomew & Son.

Bingham, H. (1988) *Learning to Live with Tourism, GCSE Resource Guide 4*, Kendal: Lake District National Park.

Black, A. and Breckwoldt, R. (1981) 'Evolution of Systems of National Park Policy–making in Australia', in D. Mercer (ed) *Outdoor Recreation: Australian Perspectives*, Malvern, Victoria: Sorrell.

Blunden, J. and Curry, N. (eds) (1990) *A People's Charter? 40 Years of the 1949 National Parks and Access to the Countryside Act*, London: HMSO.

Boden, R. and Baines G. (1981) 'National Parks in Australia–Origins and Future Trends', in D. Mercer (ed) *Outdoor Recreation: Australian Perspectives*, Malvern, Victoria: Sorrell.

Bolton, N. and Chalkey, B. (1990) 'The Rural Population Turnaround', *Journal of Rural Studies* **16**, 1: 29–43.

Bonnetaud, D. (1993) 'On the Subject of Marketing.../ A propos de la Commercialisation...', *Espaces* **119**: 15–17.

Bord Fáilte (1996) *Tourism Facts 1995*, Dublin: Bord Fáilte.

Bouquet, M. and Winter, M. (1987) *Who From Their Labours Rest? Conflict and Practice in Rural Tourism*, Aldershot: Avebury.

Bovaird, A., Tricker, M. and Stoakes, R. (1984) *Recreation Management and Pricing*, Aldershot: Gower.

Bramwell, B. and Lane, B. (1993) 'Sustainable Tourism: An Evolving Global Approach', *Journal of Sustainable Tourism* **1**, 1: 1–5.

Bramwell, B. and Lane, B. (eds) (1994) *Rural Tourism and Sustainable Rural Development*, Clevedon: Channel View Publications.

Broom, G. (1992) 'Pricing the Countryside: The Context', in H. Talbot (ed) *Our Priceless Countryside: Should it be Priced?*, Proceedings of the 1991 Countryside Recreation Conference, Bristol: CRRAG: 21–33.

Brougham J. and Butler, R. (1981) 'A Segmentation Analysis of Resident Attitudes to the Social Impact of Tourism', *Annals of Tourism Research* **8**, 4: 569–590.

Budowski, G. (1976) 'Tourism and Conservation: Conflict, Co–Existence or Symbiosis?', *Environmental Conservation* 3, 1: 27–31.

Buller, H. and Hoggart, K. (1994) 'The Social Integration of British Home Owners into French Rural Communities', *Journal of Rural Studies* **10**, 2: 197–210.

Burkhart, A and Medlik, S. (1981) *Tourism: Past, Present and Future*, 2nd edition, London: Heinemann.

Burns, P. and Holden A. (1995) *Tourism: A New Perspective*, Hemel Hempstead: Prentice Hall International.

Butler, R. (1985) 'Evolution of Tourism in the Scottish Highlands', *Annals of Tourism Research* **12**, 3: 371–391.

Butler, R. (1990) 'Alternative Tourism: pious hope or trojan horse?', *Journal of Travel Research* **28**, 3: 40–45.

Butler, R. (1992) 'Alternative Tourism: The Thin End of the Wedge', in V. Smith and W. Eadington (eds) *Tourism Alternatives: Potentials and Problems in the Development of Tourism*, Philadelphia: University of Pennsylvania Press: 31–46.

Butler, R. and Clark, G. (1992) 'Tourism in Rural Areas: Canada and the United Kingdom', in I. Bowler, C. Bryant and M. Nellis (eds) *Contemporary Rural Systems in Transition, Volume 2: Economy and Society*, Wallingford: CAB International: 161–183.

Cairncross, F. (1991) *Costing the Earth*, London: Business Books Ltd.

Calatrava Requena, J. and Avilés, P. (1993) 'Tourism: An Opportunity of Disadvantaged Rural Areas?', *Leader Magazine* **4**: 6–9.

Carson, R. (1965) *Silent Spring*, Harmondsworth: Penguin.

Cater, E. and Lowman, G. (eds) (1994) *Ecotourism: A Sustainable Option?*, Chichester: John Wiley & Sons.

Cavaco, C. (1995) 'Rural Tourism: The Creation of New Tourist Spaces', in A. Montanari and A. Williams (eds) *European Tourism: Regions, Spaces and Restructuring*, Chichester: John Wiley & Sons: 129–149.

Champion, A. (1989) *Counterurbanization: The Changing Pace and Nature of Population Deconcentration*, London: Edward Arnold.

Champion, T. and Watkins, C. (eds) (1991) *People in the Countryside*, London: PCP.

Clark, G., Darrall, J., Grove-White, R., Macnaghten, P., and Urry, J. (1994) *Leisure Landscapes – Leisure, Culture and the English Countryside: Challenges and Conflicts*, London: Council for the Protection of Rural England.

Clarke, J. (1996) 'Farm Tourism', *ETB Insights*, London: English Tourist Board: D19–25.

Clawson, M. and Knetsch, J. (1966) *Economics of Outdoor Recreation*, Baltimore: Johns Hopkins Press.

Cloke, P., Philips, M. and Rankin, D. (1991) 'Middle-Class Housing Choice: Channels of Entry into Gower, South Wales' in T. Champion and C. Watkins (eds), *People in the Countryside*, London: PCP.

Coccossis, H. and Nijkamp, P. (1995) *Sustainable Tourism Development*, Aldershot: Avebury.

Cohen, E. (1972) 'Towards a Sociology of International Tourism', *Social Research* **39**: 164–182.

Cohen, E. (1974) 'Who is a Tourist? A Conceptual Clarification', *Sociological Review* **22**, 4: 527–555.

Cohen, E. (1988) 'Authenticity and Commoditisation in Tourism', *Annals of Tourism Research* **15**, 3: 371–386.

Cointat, M. (1991) 'Rural Tourism', *Tourism Recreation Research* **16**, 1: 8–9.

Colby, K. (1988) 'Public Access to Private Land: Allemansrätt in Sweden', *Landscape and Urban Planning* **15**: 253–264.

Cooper, C., Fletcher, J., Gilbert, D. and Wanhill, S. (1993) *Tourism: Principles and Practice,* London: Pitman Publishing.

Coppock, J. (1977) *Second Homes: Curse or Blessing*, Oxford: Pergamon Press.

Countryside Commission (1985) *National Countryside Recreation Survey 1984*, CCP 201, Cheltenham: Countryside Commission.

Countryside Commission (1986) *Access to the Countryside for Recreation and Sport*, CCP 217, Cheltenham: Countryside Commission.

Countryside Commission (1987a) *Policies for Enjoying the Countryside*, CCP 234, Cheltenham: Countryside Commission.

Countryside Commission (1987b) *A Compendium of Recreation Statistics 1984–1986*, CCD 16, Cheltenham: Countryside Commission.

Countryside Commission (1987c) *Public Transport to the Countryside*, CCP 227, Cheltenham: Countryside Commission.

Countryside Commission (1989a) *Welcoming Visitors to Country Parks*, CCD 40, Cheltenham: Countryside Commission.

Countryside Commission (1989b) *Planning for a Greener Countryside*, CCP 264, Cheltenham: Countryside Commission.

Countryside Commission (1990a) *1989 Addendum to Recreation Statistics 1984–1986*, Cheltenham: Countryside Commission.

Countryside Commission (1990b) *Paths, Routes and Trails: Policies and Priorities*, CCP 226, Cheltenham: Countryside Commission.

Countryside Commission (1991a) *Countryside Stewardship: An Outline*, CCP 346, Cheltenham: Countryside Commission.

Countryside Commission (1991b) *Visitors to the Countryside,* CCP341, Cheltenham: Countryside Commission.

Countryside Commission (1992) *Road Traffic and the Countryside*, CCP 387, Cheltenham: Countryside Commission.

Countryside Commission (1995a) *National Survey of Countryside Recreation 1990: Summary of Results*, Cheltenham: Countryside Commission.

Countryside Commission (1995b) *Sustainable Rural Tourism: Opportunities for Local Action*, CCP 483, Cheltenham: Countryside Commission.

Cowell, D. (1984) *The Marketing of Services*, Oxford: Butterworth Heinemann.

CPRE (1992) *The Lost Land: Land Use Change in England 1945–1990*, London: Council for the Protection of Rural England.

CRN (1994) '1993 UK Day Visits Survey: Summary', *Countryside Recreation Network News* **2**, 1: 7–12.

CRN (1995) *UK Day Visits Survey 1993*, Cardiff: Countryside Recreation Network.

Croall, J. (1995) *Preserve or Destroy: Tourism and the Environment*, London: Calouste Gulbenkian Foundation.

Crocker, S. (1986) 'Diversification: Pitfalls or Profit?', *Journal of the Royal Agricultural Society of England* **146**, 1: 26–33.

CTO (1991) *Agrotourism*, Information Sheet, Nicosia: Cyprus Tourism Organisation.

Cullen, R. (1985) 'Rationing Recreation Use of Public Land', *Journal of Environmental Management* **21**: 213–224.

Curry, N. (1994) *Countryside Recreation, Access and Land Use Planning*, London: E. & F.N. Spon.

Curry, N. (1996) 'Access: Policy Directions for the Late 1990s', in C. Watkins (ed), *Rights of Way: Policy, Culture and Mangement*, London: Pinter: 24–34.

Dann, G. (1981) 'Tourist Motivation: An Appraisal', *Annals of Tourism Research* **8**, 2: 187–219.

Davidson, R. (1992) *Tourism in Europe*, London: Pitman Publishing.

Dean, K., Shaw, D., Brown, B., Perry, R. and Thorneycroft, W. (1984) 'Counterurbanisation and the Characteristics of Persons Migrating to West Cornwall', *Geoforum* **15**, 2: 177–190.

Dearden, P. and Rollins, R. (1993) *Parks and Protected Areas in Canada: Planning and Management*, Toronto: OUP.

Deegan, J. and Dineen, D. (1993) 'Employment Effects of Irish Tourism Projects: A Microeconomic Approach', in P. Johnson and B. Thomas (eds) *Perspectives on Tourism Policy*, London: Mansell: 137–156.

Denman, R. and Denman, J. (1993) *The Farm Tourism Market: a Market Study of Farm Tourism in England*, Ledbury: The Tourism Company.

Dernoi, L. (1991) 'About Rural and Farm Tourism', *Tourism Recreation Research* **16**, 1: 3–6.

Devon County Council (1988) *The Tarka Project – an Integrated Conservation, Recreation and Tourism Strategy for North Devon*, Exeter: Devon CC.

Devon County Council (1993) *Tarka Project: Options for the Future*, Consultation Document, Exeter: Devon CC.

Dowling, R. (1993) 'An Environmentally-based Planning Model for Regional Tourism Development', *Journal of Sustainable Tourism* **1**, 1: 17–37.

Dwyer, J. (1994) *Customer Diversity and the Future Demand for Outdoor Recreation*, Fort Collins: USDA Forest Service.

Edwards, R. (Chairman) (1991) *Fit for the Future, Report of the National Parks Review Panel*, CCP334, Cheltenham: Countryside Commission.

EIU (1992) 'Cyprus', *International Tourism Reports No 2*, London: Economic Intelligence Unit: 43–64.

EIU (1991) 'Republic of Ireland', *International Tourism Reports No 4*, London: Economic Intelligence Unit: 25–45.

Embacher, H. (1994) 'Marketing for Agri-tourism in Austria: Strategy and Realisation in a Highly Developed Tourist Destination', in B. Bramwell and B. Lane (eds) *Rural Tourism and Sustainable Rural Development*, Clevedon: Channel View Publications: 61–76.

ETB (1988) *Visitors in the Countryside: A Development Strategy*, London: English Tourist Board.

ETB (1991) *The Green Light: A Guide to Sustainable Tourism*, London: English Tourist Board.

ETB/Countryside Commission (1989) *Principles for Tourism in the Countryside*, London: ETB/Countryside Commission.

ETB/CTB (1995) *Regional Tourism Facts: Cumbria*, London: English Tourist Board/Cumbria Tourist Board.

ETB/DoE (1991) *Tourism and the Environment: Maintaining the Balance*, London: English Tourist Board/Department of the Environment.

Fagence, M. (1991) 'Rural Tourism and the Small Country Town', *Tourism Recreation Reserarch* **16**, 1: 34–48.

Fairbrother, N. (1972) *New Lives, New Landscapes*, Harmondsworth: Penguin.

Fitton, M. (1979) 'Countryside Recreation: the Problems of Opportunity', *Local Government Studies* 5: 57–90.

Flint, D. (1992) *Tourism in Europe*, Hove: Wayland.

FNNPE (1993) *Loving Them to Death? Sustainable Tourism in Europe's Nature and National Parks*, Grafenau: Federation of National and Nature Parks of Europe.

Forestry Commission (1993) *Forest Enterprise Corporate Agenda 1993–1994*, Edinburgh: Forestry Commission.

Fractor, D. (1982) 'Evaluating Alternative Methods for Rationing Wilderness Use', *Journal of Leisure Research* **14**, 4: 341–349.

Frater, J. (1983) 'Farm Tourism in England: Planning, Funding, Promotion and Some Lessons from Europe', *Tourism Management* **4**, 3: 167–179.

Fuller, A. (1990) 'From Part-Time Farming to Pluriactivity: a Decade of Change in Rural Europe', *Journal of Rural Studies* **6**, 4: 361–373.

Gammon, S. (1996) *Leisure, Migration and the Stagnant Village*, paper presented at the Leisure, Time and Space Conference, Wageningen, Netherlands.

Gannon, A. (1994) 'Rural Tourism as a Factor in Rural Community Economic Development for Economies in Transition', in B. Bramwell and B. Lane (eds) *Rural Tourism and Sustainable Rural Development*, Clevedon: Channel View Publications: 51–60

Garner, J. and Jones, B. (1993) *Countryside Law,* 2nd edition, London: Shaw & Sons.

Getz, D. and Jamal, T. (1994) 'The Environment-Community Symbiosis: A Case for Collaborative Tourism Planning', *Journal of Sustainable Tourism* **2**, 3: 152–173.

Gilbert, D. (1989) 'Rural Tourism and Marketing: Synthesis and new ways of working', *Tourism Management*, **10**, 1: 39–50.

Gilbert, D. (1990) 'Conceptual Issues in the Meaning of Tourism', in C. Cooper (ed) *Progress in Tourism, Recreation and Hospitality Management*, London: Bellhaven Press: 4–27.

Gilbert, D. and Tung, L. (1990) 'Public Organisations and Rural Marketing Planning in England and Wales', *Tourism Management*, **11**, 3: 164–172.

Gilg, A. (1991) 'Switzerland: Structural Change Within Stability', in A. Williams and G. Shaw (eds) *Tourism & Economic Development: Western European Experiences*, London: Bellhaven Press: 130–152.

Gillmor, D. (1994) 'Tourism Development and Impact in the Republic of Ireland', in U. Kockel (ed) *Culture, Tourism and Development: The Case of Ireland*, Liverpool: Liverpool University Press:17–34.

Glyptis, S. (1991) *Countryside Recreation*, Harlow: Longman/ILAM.

Glyptis, S. (ed) (1993) *Leisure and the Environment, Essays in Honour of Professor J Patmore*, London: Bellhaven Press.

Gold, J. and Ward, S. (eds) (1994) *Place Promotion: The Use of Publicity and Marketing to Sell Towns and Regions*, Chichester: John Wiley & Sons.

Goodall, B. (1991) 'Understanding Holiday Choice', in C. Cooper (ed) *Progress in Tourism, Recreation and Hospitality Management Volume 3*, London: Bellhaven Press: 58–77.

Grahn, P. (1991) 'Using Tourism to Protect Existing Culture: A Project in Swedish Lapland', *Leisure Studies* **10**, 1: 33–47.

Greffe, X. (1994) 'Is Rural Tourism a Lever for Economic and Social Development?', in B. Bramwell and B. Lane (eds) *Rural Tourism and Sustainable Rural Development*, Clevedon: Channel View Publications: 22–46.

Grolleau, H. (1987) *Rural Tourism in the 12 Member States of the European Economic Community*, EEC Tourism Unit, DG XXIII.

Gunn, C. (1994) *Tourism Planning: Basics, Concepts, Cases,* 3rd edition, London: Taylor & Francis Ltd.

Halfacree, K. (1995) 'Talking about Rurality: Social Representations of the Rural as Expressed by Residents of Six English Parishes', *Journal of Rural Studies* **11**, 1: 1–20.

Halfacree, K. (1993) 'Locality and Social Representation: Space, Discourse, and Alternative Definitions of the Rural', *Journal of Rural Studies* **9**, 1: 23–37.

Hanley, N. (1989) 'Valuing Rural Recreation Benefits: An Empirical Comparison of Two Approaches', *Journal of Agricultural Economics* **40**, 3: 361–374.

Hannigan, K. (1994a) 'A Regional Analysis of Tourism Growth in Ireland', *Regional Studies* **28**, 2: 208–214.

Hannigan, K. (1994b) 'National Policy, European Structural Funds and Sustainable Tourism: The Case of Ireland', *Journal of Sustainable Tourism* **2**, 4: 179–192.

Harris, C. and Driver, B. (1987) 'Recreation User Fees – Pros and Cons', *Journal of Forestry* **85**, 5: 25–29.

Harrison, C. (1991) *Countryide Recreation in a Changing Society*, London: TMS Partnership.

Harrison, C., Limb, M. and Burgess, J. (1986) *Popular Values for the Countryside*, London: UCL.

Haywood, K.M. (1988) 'Responsible and Responsive Tourism Planning in the Community', *Tourism Management* **9**: 105–118.

Hewison, R. (1987) *The Heritage Industry: Britain in a Climate of Decline*, London: Methuen.

Hewison, R. (1989) 'Heritage: an Interpretation', in D. Uzzell (ed) *Heritage InterpretationVolume 1, The Natural & Built Environment*, London: Bellhaven Press:15–23.

Hill, B. (1992) 'Sustainable Tourism', *Parks and Recreation* **27**, 9: 84–89.

Hill, H. (1980) *Freedom to Roam: the Struggle for Access to Britain's Moors and Mountains*, Ashbourne: Moorland Publishing.

HMSO (1996) *Regional Trends 1996 Edition*, National Statistics Office, London: HMSO.

Hoggart, K., Buller, H. and Black, R.(1995), *Rural Europe: Identity and Change*, London: Arnold.

Holland, S. and Crotts, J. (1992) 'A Strategic Planning Approach to Tourism Development in Rural Communities', *Visions in Leisure and Business* **11**, 1: 14–23.

Holloway, J.C. (1994) *The Business of Tourism,* 4th edition, London: Pitman Publishing.

Holloway, J. C. and Plant R. (1992) *Marketing for Tourism,* 2nd edition, London: Pitman Publishing.

Hoyland, I. (1982) 'The Development of Farm Tourism in the UK and Europe', *Farm Management* **4**, 10: 383–389.

Hummelbrunner, R. and Miglbauer, E. (1994) 'Tourism Promotion and Potential in Peripheral Areas: The Austrian Case', in B. Bramwell and B. Lane (eds) *Rural Tourism and Sustainable Rural Development*, Clevedon: Channel View Publications: 41–50.

Hunter, C. and Green, H. (1995) *Tourism and the Environment: A Sustainable Relationship?*, London: Routledge.

Hurley, A., Archer, B. and Fletcher, J. (1994) 'The Economic Impact of European Community Grants for Tourism in the Republic of Ireland', *Tourism Management* **15**, 3: 203–211.

Hvenegaard, G. (1994) 'Ecotourism: A Status Report and Conceptual Framework', *Journal of Tourism Studies* **5**, 2: 24–35.

Inskeep, E. (1991) *Tourism Planning: an Integrated and Sustainable Development Approach*, New York: Van Nostrand Reinhold.

Ioannides, D. (1995) 'A Flawed Implementation of Sustainable Tourism: The Experience of Akamas, Cyprus', *Tourism Management* **16**, 8: 583–592.

IUCN (1975) *World Directory of National Parks and Other Protected Areas*, International Union for the Conservation of Nature and Natural Resources.

Jansen-Verbeke, M. and Nijmegen, K. (1990) 'The Potentials of Rural Tourism and Agritourism', *Problemy Turystyki* **13**, 1–2: 35–47.

Jefferson, A. and Lickorish, L. (1988) *Marketing Tourism: A Practical Guide*, Harlow: Longman.

Jim, C. (1989) 'Visitor Management in Recreation Areas', *Environmental Conservation* **16**, 1: 19–34.

Jones, H., Caird, J., Berry, W. and Dewhurst, J. (1986) 'Peripheral Counter-Urbanization: Findings from an Integration of Census and Survey Data in Northern Scotland', *Regional Studies* **20**, 1: 15–26.

Jones, P. (1990) 'Lakes Being 'Loved to Death'', *Farmers Weekly*, 9 February: 50–57.

Juez, R. (1991) 'Creative Re-Use of Heritage Buildings in Tourism –The Paradores of Spain as a Model', in *New Forms of Demand and New Products*, Madrid: World Tourism Organisation.

de Kadt, E. (1979) *Tourism: Passport to Development?*, Oxford: OUP.

Kieselbach, S. and Long, P. (1990) 'Tourism and the Rural Revitalization Movement', *Parks and Recreation* **25**, 3: 62–66.

Kinsman, P. (1996) 'Conflict and Co-operation over Ethnic Minority Access to the Countryside: The Black Environment Network and the Countryside Commission', in C. Watkins (ed), *Rights of Way: Policy, Culture and Mangement*, London: Pinter: 162–178.

Kockel, U. (ed) (1994) *Culture, Tourism and Development. The Case of Ireland*, Liverpool University Press.

Kotler, P. (1975) *Marketing for Non-Profit Organisations*, Englewood Cliffs: Prentice Hall.

Kotler, P. (1991) *Marketing Management: Analysis, Planning, Implementation and Control,* 7th edition, Hemel Hempstead: Prentice Hall International.

Kotler, P., Haider, D. and Rein, I. (1993) *Marketing Places*, New York: Free Press.

Krippendorf, J. (1987) *The Holidaymakers*, Oxford: Heinemann.

Lane, B. (1994a) 'What is Rural Tourism?' in B. Bramwell and B. Lane (eds) *Rural Tourism and Sustainable Rural Development*, Clevedon: Channel View Publications: 7–21.

Lane, B. (1994b) 'Sustainable Rural Tourism Strategies: A Tool for Development and Conservation', in B. Bramwell and B. Lane (eds) *Rural Tourism and Sustainable Rural Development*, Clevedon: Channel View Publications: 102–111.

Lankford, S. (1994) 'Attitudes and Perceptions Towards Tourism and Rural Regional Development', *Journal of Travel Research* **32**, 3: 35–43.

Leuschner, W., Cook, D., Roggenbuck, J. and Oderwald, R. (1987) 'A Comparative Analysis for Wilderness User Fee Policy', *Journal of Leisure Research* **19**, 2: 102–115.

Liu, J., Sheldon, P. and Var, T. (1987) 'Resident Perceptions of the Environmental Impacts of Tourism', *Annals of Tourism Research* **14**, 1: 17–37.

Long, V. (1993) 'Techniques for Socially Sustainable Tourism Development: Lessons from Mexico', in J. Nelson, R. Butler and G. Wall (eds) *Tourism and Sustainable Development: Monitoring, Planning, Managing*, University of Waterloo: 201–218.

Lowe, P. and Goyder, J. (1983) *Environmental Groups in Politics*, London: George Allen & Unwin.

Lowenthal. D. and Prince, H. (1965) 'English Landscape Tastes', *Geographical Review* 55: 186–222.

Lowyck, E., Van Langenhove, L. and Bollaert, L. (1992) 'Typologies of Tourist Roles', in P. Johnson and B. Thomas (eds) *Choice and Demand in Tourism*, London: Mansell: 13–32.

Luloff, A., Bridger, J., Graefe, A., Saylor, M., Martin, K. and Gitelson, R. (1994) 'Assessing Rural Tourism Efforts in the United States', *Annals of Tourism Research* **21**, 1: 46–64.

MacCannell, D. (1989) *The Tourist: A New Theory of the Leisure Class,* 2nd edition, New York: Shocken Books.

MacEwan, M. and MacEwan, A. (1982) *National Parks: Conservation or Cosmetics?*, London: George Allen and Unwin.

MacEwan, M. and MacEwan, A. (1987) *Greenprints for the Countryside? The Story of Britain's National Parks*, London: George Allen and Unwin.

Mansfeld, Y. (1992) 'From Motivation to Actual Travel', *Annals of Tourism Research* **19**, 3: 399–419.

Marsden, T., Murdoch, J., Lowe, P., Munton, R. and Flynn, A. (1993) *Constructing the Countryside*, London: UCL Press.

Marsh, J. (1987) 'National Parks and Tourism in Small Developing Countries', in S. Britton and W. Clarke (eds) *Ambiguous Alternative: Tourism in Small Developing Countries*, Suva: University of the South Pacific: 25–45.

Mathieson, A. and Wall, G. (1982) *Tourism: Economic, Physical and Social Impacts*, Harlow: Longman.

Maude, A. and van Rest, D. (1985) 'The Social and Economic Effects of Farm Tourism in the United Kingdom', *Agriculrural Administration* 20: 85–99.

McCallum, J. and Adams, J. (1980) 'Charging for Countryside Recreation: A Review with Implications for Scotland', *Transactions of the Institute of British Geographers* 5: 350–368.

McCormack, F. (1994) *Water Based Recreation: Managing Water Resources for Leisure*, Huntingdon: Elm Publications.

McKercher, B. (1993) 'Can Tourism Survive 'Sustainability'?', *Tourism Management*, **14**, 2: 131–136.

McNamee, K. (1993) 'From Wild Places to Endangered Species: A History of Canada's National Parks', in P. Dearden and R. Rollins (eds) *Parks and Protected Areas in Canada: Planning and Management*, Toronto: OUP.

Medlik, S. and Middleton, V. (1973) 'The Tourist Product and its Marketing Implications', *International Tourism Quarterly*, 3: 28–35.

Middleton, V. (1988) *Marketing in Travel and Tourism*, Oxford: Heinemann.

Middleton, V. (1995) 'Managing the Marketing Mix: Overall Tourism Product', in S. Witt and L. Mouthino (eds), *Tourism Marketing and Management Handbook, Student Edition*, Hemel Hempstead: Prentice Hall International: 334–341.

Middleton, V. (1996) 'Sustainable Tourism: A Marketing Perspective', Proceedings of *Sustainable Tourism – Ethics, Economics and the Environment Conference*, Newton Rigg, Cumbria.

Middleton, V. and Hawkins, R. (1993) 'Practical Environmental Policies in Travel and Tourism – Part 1: The Hotel Sector', *Travel & Tourism Analyst* 6: 63–76.

Mieczkowski, Z. (1995) *Environmental Issues of Tourism and Recreation*, Lanham: University Press of America.

Millward, H. (1992) 'Public Access in the Canadian Countryside: A Comparative Survey', *Canadian Geographer* 36: 30–44.

Millward, H. (1993) 'Public Access in the West European Countryside: A Comparative Survey', *Journal of Rural Studies* **9**, 1: 39–51.

Mitchell, J. (1991) *Tourism and Public Transport in National Parks*, unpublished MSc thesis, University of Strathclyde.

Murdoch, J. and Pratt, A. (1993) 'Rural Studies: Modernism, Postmodernism and the Post-rural', *Journal of Rural Studies* **9**, 4: 411–427.

Murphy, P. (1983) 'Tourism as a Community Industry: an Ecological Model of Tourism Development, *Tourism Management*, **4**, 3: 180–193.

Murphy, P. (1985) *Tourism: A Community Approach*, London: Routledge.

Nash, D. (1981) 'Tourism as an Anthropological Subject', *Current Anthropology* **22**, 5: 461–481.

Nelson, J., Butler, R. and Wall, G. (1993) *Tourism and Sustainable Development: Monitoring, Planning, Managing*, University of Waterloo.

Newby, H. (1985) *Green and Pleasant Land? Social Change in Rural England*, London, Wildwood House.

Newby, H. (1986) 'Locality and Rurality: The Restructuring of Rural Social Relations' *Regional Studies* **20**, 3: 209–215.

Nitsch, B. and van Straaten, J. (1995) 'Rural Tourism Development: Using a Sustainable Tourism Development Approach', in H. Coccossis and P. Nijkamp (eds), *Sustainable Tourism Development*, Aldershot: Avebury: 169–185.

Norton, G. (1992) *Resource Economics*, London: Edward Arnold.

Nugent, N. (1994) *The Government and Politics of the European Union*, 3rd edition, Basingstoke: Macmillan.

Nuñez, T. (1989) 'Touristic Studies in Anthropological Perspective', in V. Smith (ed) *Hosts and Guests: The Anthropology of Tourism*, 2nd edition, Philadelphia: University of Pennsylvania Press: 265–279.

OECD (1991) *Environmental Indicators*, Paris: OECD.

OECD (1993) *What Future For Our Countryside? A Rural Development Policy*, Paris: OECD.

OECD (1994) *Tourism Policy and International Tourism in OECD Countries 1991–1992*, Paris: OECD.

Olwig, K. (1989) 'Nature Interpretation: A Threat to the Countryside', in D. Uzzell (ed) *Heritage InterpretationVolume 1, The Natural & Built Environment*, London: Bellhaven Press:132–141.

Oppermann, M. (1996) 'Rural Tourism in Southern Germany', *Annals of Tourism Research* **23**, 1: 86–102.

Page, S. (1994) 'Perspectives on Tourism and Peripherality: a Review of Tourism in the Republic of Ireland', in C. Cooper and A. Lockwood (eds) *Progress in Tourism, Recreation and Hospitality Management Volume 5*, London: Bellhaven Press: 26–53.

Parrinello, G. (1993) 'Motivation and Anticipation in Post–Industrial Tourism', *Annals of Tourism Research* **20**, 2: 233–249.

Pearce, D. (1989) *Tourist Development,* 2nd edition, Harlow: Longman.

Pearce, D. (1993) *Blueprint 3*, London: Earthscan Publications.

Pearce, D., Markandya, A. and Barbier, E. (1989) *Blueprint for a Green Economy,* London: Earthscan Publications.

Peattie, K. (1992) *Green Marketing*, M+E Handbooks, London: Pitman Publishing.

Perdue, R., Long, P. and Allen, L. (1987) 'Rural Resident Tourism Perceptions and Attitudes', *Annals of Tourism Research*, 14: 420–429.

Perry, R., Dean, K. and Brown, B. (1986) *Counterurbanisation: International Case Studies of Socio–Economic Change in Rural Areas*, Norwich: Geo Books.

Phillips, A. (1989) 'Interpreting the Countryside and the Natural Environment, in D. Uzzell (ed) *Heritage InterpretationVolume 1, The Natural & Built Environment*, London. Bellhaven Press: 121–131.

Pichler, G. (1991) 'Agri-Tourism (Farm Holidays) in Austria, in *New Forms of Demand and New Products*, Madrid: World Tourism Organisation: 92–96.

Pigram, J. (1983) *Outdoor Recreation and Resource Management*, Beckenham: Croom Helm.

Pigram, J. (1993) 'Planning for Tourism in Rural Areas: Bridging the Policy Implementation Gap', in D. Pearce and R. Butler (eds) *Tourism Reseach: Critiques and Challenges*, London: Routledge: 156–174.

Pizam, A. (1978) 'Tourism's Impacts: The Social Cost to the Destination Community as Perceived by its Residents', *Journal of Travel Research* **16**, 4: 8–12.

Plog, S. (1977) 'Why Destination Areas Rise and Fall in Popularity', in E. Kelly (ed) *Domestic and International Tourism*, Wellesley, MA: Institute of Certified Travel Agents.

Pompl, W. and Lavery, P. (1993) *Tourism in Europe: Structures and Developments*, Wallingford: CAB International.

Poon, A. (1993) *Tourism, Technology and Competitive Strategies*, Wallingford: CAB International.

Porritt, J. (1995) Keynote Speech, *Managing Tourism: Education and Regulation for Sustainability Symposium*, London: Commonwealth Institute.

Potts, T., Backman, K., Uysal, M. and Backman, S. (1992) 'Issues in Rural Community Tourism Development, *Visions in Leisure and Business*, **11**, 1: 5–13.

Ravenscroft, N. (1996) 'New Access Initiatives: The Extension of Recreation Opportunities or the Diminution of Citizen Rights?', in C. Watkins (ed), *Rights of Way: Policy, Culture and Mangement*, London: Pinter: 35–48.

Roberts, L. (1996) 'Barriers to the Development of Rural Tourism in the Bran Area of Transylvania, in M. Robinson, N. Evans and P. Callaghan (eds), *Tourism and Culture; Image, Identity and Marketing*, Sunderland: Business Education Publishers;185–196.

Rollinson, W. (1967) *A History of Man in the Lake District*, London: J.M. Dent & Sons.

Ross, G. (1992) 'Resident Perceptions of the Impact of Tourism on an Australian City', *Journal of Travel Research*, **30**, 3: 13–17.

Ryan, C. (1991) *Recreational Tourism: A Social Science Perspective*, London: Routledge.

Sandell, K. (1995) 'Access to the 'North' – But to What and for Whom? Public Access in the Swedish Countryside and the Case of a Proposed National Park in the Kiruna Mountains', in C.M. Hall and M. Johnston (eds) *Polar Tourism– Tourism in the Arctic and Antarctic Regions*, Chichester: John Wiley & Sons: 131–145.

Scott, P. (1992) 'Access to Open Countryside – A European Perspective', in *Off the Beaten Track*, Cardiff: Countryside Recreation Network.

Sharpley, R. (1993) 'Sustainable Tourism in the English Countryside – Should the User Pay?', *Sustainable Development*, **1**, 3: 49–63.

Sharpley, R. (1994) *Tourism, Tourists and Society*, Huntingdon: Elm Publications.

Sharpley, R. (1996) *Tourism and Leisure in the Countryside,* 2nd edition, Huntingdon: Elm Publications.

Shaw, G. and Williams, A. (1994) *Critical Issues in Tourism: A Geographical Perspective*, Oxford: Blackwell.

Shoard, M. (1980) *The Theft of the Countryside*, London: Temple Smith.

Shoard, M. (1987) *This Land is Our Land*, London: Paladin.

Shoard, M. (1996) 'Robbers v. Revolutionaries: what the Battle for Access is Really All About', in C. Watkins (ed), *Rights of Way: Policy, Culture and Mangement*, London: Pinter: 11–23.

Short, J. (1991) *Imagined Country: Society, Culture and Environment*, London: Routledge.

Sidaway, R. (1988) *Sport, Recreation and Nature Conservation*, London: Sports Council.

Silver, I. (1993) 'Marketing Authenticity in Third World Countries', *Annals of Tourism Research* **20**, 2: 303–318.

Sinclair, D. (1990) *Shades of Green: Myth and Muddle in the Countryside*, London: Paladin.

Slee, R. and Yells, R. (1984/85) 'Some Aspects of Marketing Farm Holiday Accommodation', *Farm Management* **5**, 8:317–323.

Smith, V. (ed) (1989) *Hosts and Guests: The Anthropology of Tourism,* 2nd edition, Philadelphia: University of Pennsylvania Press.

Smith, V. and Eadington, W. (1992) *Tourism Alternatives: Potentials and Problems in the Development of Tourism*, Philadelphia: University of Pennsylvania Press.

Sports Council (1990) *A Countryside for Sport: Towards a Policy for Sport and Recreation in the Countryside*, Consultation Document, London: Sports Council.

Squire, S. (1994) 'The Cultural Values of Literary Tourism', *Annals of Tourism Research* **21**, 1: 103–120.

Stevens, T. (1989) 'The Visitor – Who Cares? Interpretation and Consumer Relations', in D. Uzzell (ed) *Heritage Interpretation Volume 2: The Visitor Experience*, London: Bellahven Press: 103–109.

Stokes, R. (1989) 'National Parks – Who Pays?', *Environmental Education and Information* **8**, 4: 225–235.

Szabo, L. (1991) 'Prospects of Rural Tourism in Transylvania (Romania)', *Tourism Recreation Research* **16**, 1: 29–32.

Tanner, M. (1993) 'Recreation, Conservation and the Changing Management of Water Resources in England and Wales', in S. Glyptis (ed), *Leisure and the Environment, Essays in Honour of Professor J. Patmore*, London: Bellhaven Press: 96–115.

Thibal, S. (1988) *Rural Tourism in Europe*, Strasbourg: Council of Europe.

Towner, J. (1985) 'The Grand Tour: A Key Phase in the History of Tourism', *Annals of Tourism Research*, **12**, 3: 297–333.

Transport 2000 (1989) *No Through Road*, London: Transport 2000.

Turner, L. and Ash, J. (1975) *The Golden Hordes: International Tourism and the Pleasure Periphery*, London: Constable.

Turner, R (1993) *Sustainable Economics and Management*, London: Bellhaven Press.

Turnock, D. (1990) 'Tourism in Romania: Rural Planning in the Carpathians', *Annals of Tourism Research* **17**, 1: 79–102.

Turnock, D. (1991) 'Romania', in D. Hall (ed) *Tourism and Economic Development in Eastern Europe and the Soviet Union*, London: Bellhaven Press: 203–219.

Urry, J. (1990a) *The Tourist Gaze*, London: Sage Publications.

Urry, J. (1990b) 'The Consumption of Tourism', *Sociology* **24**, 1: 23–35.

Utah (1995) *1994 Economic and Travel Industry Profiles for Utah Counties*, Division of Travel Development, Utah Dept of Community and Economic Development.

Uzzell, D. (ed) (1989) *Heritage Interpretation Volume 1: The Natural and Built Environment*, London: Bellhaven Press.

Valenzuela, M. (1991) 'Spain: the Phenomenon of Mass Tourism', in A. Williams and G. Shaw (eds) *Tourism & Economic Development: Western European Experiences*, London: Bellhaven Press: 40–60.

Vaux, H (1975) 'The Distribution of Income among Wilderness Users', *Journal of Leisure Research*, **7**,1: 29–37.

Walsh, R. (1986) *Recreation Economic Decisions*, State College, Pennsylvania: Venture Publishing.

Walter, J. (1982) 'Social Limits to Tourism', *Leisure Studies* 1: 295–304.

Waters, G. (1994) 'Government Policies for the Countryside', *Land Use Policy* **11**, 2: 88–93.

WCED (1987) *Our Common Future*, The World Commission on Environment and Development, Oxford: OUP.

Weideger, P. (1994) *Gilding the Acorn: Behind the Facade of the National Trust*, London: Simon & Schuster.

Wheeller, B. (1992a) 'Is Progressive Tourism Appropriate?', *Tourism Management* **13**, 1: 104–105.

Wheeller, B. (1992b) 'Alternative Tourism: A Deceptive Ploy', in C. Cooper and A. Lockwood (eds) *Progress in Tourism, Recreation and Hospitality Management Volume 4*, London: Bellhaven Press: 140–145.

Whelan, T. (ed) (1991) *Nature Tourism: Managing for the Environment*, Washington DC: Island Press.

Whitelegg, J. (1993) *Transport for a Sustainable Future: The Case for Europe*, London: Bellhaven Press.

Wilkinson, P. (1978) The Global Distribution of National Parks and Equivalent Reserves, in J. Nelson, R. Needham and D. Mann (eds) *International Experience with National Parks and Related Reserves*, University of Waterloo.

Williams, A. and Shaw, G. (1991) *Tourism & Economic Development: Western European Experiences,* 2nd edition, London: Bellhaven Press.

Williams, R. (1985) *The Country and the City*, London: Hogarth Press.

Wood, K. and House, S. (1991) *The Good Tourist: A Worldwide Guide for the Green Traveller*, London: Mandarin.

Woodley, A. (1993) 'Tourism and Sustainable Development: The Community Perspective', in J. Nelson, R. Butler and G. Wall.(eds) *Tourism and Sustainable Development: Monitoring, Planning, Managing*, University of Waterloo:135–148.

Wright, P. (1985) *On Living in an Old Country*, London: Verso.

WTO (1993) *Sustainable Tourism Development: Guide for Local Planners*, Madrid: World Tourism Organisation.

WTO (1994) *National and Regional Tourism Planning: Methodologies and Case Studies*, London: World Tourism Organisation and Routledge.

WTO (1995) *Yearbook of Tourism Statistics*, Madrid: World Tourism Organisation.

WTTC (1994) *Travel and Tourism: Progress and Priorities 1994*, Brussels: World Travel and Tourism Council.

Yale, P. (1991) *From Tourist Attractions to Heritage Tourism*, Huntingdon: Elm Publications.

Yiordamli, A. (1995) 'The Starry Eyed Need Not Apply', *In Focus* 16, Tourism Concern: 11–12.

Young, Sir G. (1973) *Tourism: Blessing or Blight?*, Harmondsworth: Penguin.

Zube, E. and Galante, J. (1994) 'Marketing Landscapes of the Four Corners States', in J. Gold and S. Ward (eds) *Place Promotion: The Use of Publicity and Marketing to Sell Towns and Regions*, Chichester: John Wiley & Sons: 213–232.

Index